HISTORIC
INNS
ALONG THE
RIVER
THAMES

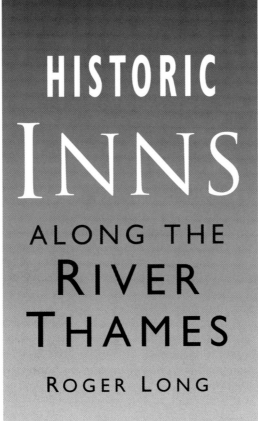

HISTORIC
INNS
ALONG THE
RIVER
THAMES

Roger Long

SUTTON PUBLISHING

Sutton Publishing Limited
Phoenix Mill · Thrupp · Stroud
Gloucestershire · GL5 2BU

First published 2006

British Library Cataloguing in Publication Data
A catalogue record for this book is available from the
British Library.

ISBN 0-7509-4364-5

Typeset in 10.5/13.5 Photina.
Typesetting and origination by
Sutton Publishing Limited.
Printed and bound in England by
J.H. Haynes & Co. Ltd, Sparkford.

CONTENTS

PREFACE

It is said that confidence is what one has before knowing the full facts of a case. I listed, mapped out and visited 220 pubs while researching this book, working from source to sea. The information was not easy to glean. I must admit to having experienced some feelings of frustration after enquiring at many ancient inns that were outwardly promising, only to find that their landlords knew nothing of their histories. Many of these enchanting places are now owned by conglomerates that heartlessly stamp their own insignia of uniformity on the premises. Individuality does not sit well with sharpened commerce. I questioned many a busy manager who knew nothing of his premises, and enquired despairingly of countless bar staff whose first language was Serbo-Croat, or some other East European tongue. I knew from prior experience that to write to the breweries for information would be pointless; and so I began to realise the nature and challenge of my task.

I resorted to researching hundreds of old books, newspapers, magazines and library records. I also extend my Thames-side to include several hostelries in the towns and villages through which the river runs. But I promise that none of the inns mentioned in this book is more than a good stone's throw from the waterside. I also had to compromise a little where age is concerned, for I found many a beautiful old inn that had no story to tell. A writer on a mission such as mine would be dull indeed if he repeatedly described old beams, flagstone floors, inglenooks, horse brasses and warming pans – when, a few yards down the road, a slightly newer establishment might have witnessed a sensational murder.

I have also avoided describing the culinary and liquid delights of the inns. There are specialist books describing these and other pub facilities, and they do a fine job.

This is a book of stories, of allegedly true tales associated with the inns. There are romantic details about authors, poets and artists, a couple of truly horrific stories, several haunting tales, legends of courageous heroes, stories ribald or comical, together with some colourful anecdotes of charismatic landlords, tales of highwaymen and love stories concerning the elopements of landlords' daughters. Historical accounts of royal patrons also put in an appearance. Jerome K. Jerome is mentioned, with his *Three Men in a Boat*. The kids are not forgotten either, for what could be more representative of the Thames in summer than Kenneth Grahame's Toad, Mole and Ratty?

I could go on for ever, but I shall not.

As ever, I trust that this book gives its readers as much pleasure as I gained from researching it.

Roger Long

THE PUBS
From Source to Sea

THAMES HEAD: *THAMES HEAD INN*

The Thames Head Inn lies beside the A433 Cirencester–Tetbury road,
3–4 miles south-west of Cirencester.

The Thames Head is almost certainly the nearest hostelry to the source of the Thames, and as such marks the starting point of my journey. The disputed start of the Thames lies a couple of fields away, marked by a simple monument and a small stone.

It is strange how things become stuck in one's mind. I cannot visit the source of this mighty river without remembering a television skit. The Hero, possibly Monty Python, made his way with an intrepid team to the source. There they discovered a dripping tap. I believe they changed the washer. The next scene was a view of Oxford

bisected by a dried-up river bed. Oxford was swiftly followed by Reading, Windsor, Staines, Richmond and London. The skit culminated at a dried-up seabed near Southend.

Back to the Thames Head Inn. It is an attractive pub, but knows little of its history. Its position beside the A429 ensures its popularity with passing trade. The interior is tasteful, antiquated and spacious. What a figure of Dick Turpin was doing here I neither knew nor enquired. I ordered some victuals and meandered outside to take a photograph. Old Father Thames adorned the signboard and the walls. Behind the main building is a stable or barn that seems centuries older than the inn, and probably has its own unknown story.

The Thames Head advertises 'Traditional Ales and Fine Food'. No empty claim is this. Ask one who engaged greedily in the partaking of both.

CRICKLADE: *RED LION*

The Red Lion is situated in the main street at Cricklade. The village is just off the A419, the Swindon-to-Cirencester road.

This is a gem of an inn, one of many that line the main street of this quaint little town. Cricklade is as old as the hills. There were Roman camps here, and the mighty Ermine Street encircled the area. This was very handy when the bypass was constructed many centuries later. It is probably as a result of the bypass that the little town has remained intact and kept its original character. The Red Lion stands a short distance from the narrow river (even I could swim across it here). Its date of

birth is undecided, as parts of it have been rebuilt, but there is thought to have been some kind of hostelry here since the sixteenth century.

Inside, the Red Lion looks like a classy and well-stocked antique shop. Animals' heads protrude from every wall and stuffed birds and creatures adorn every corner, lorded over by a massive concrete lion's head. I took a chair directly under a stuffed squirrel that seemed to have rammed its head into a can of a popular lager. There are perhaps a dozen clocks in the room, all meticulously wound, and all telling the right time. However, it has not always been so. One strange night they all stopped at two o'clock. Electric, clockwork and pendulum – all ceased to function at precisely the same time. Could it have been something to do with the ghostly old lady who occasionally appears?

But that is another story.

CRICKLADE: *WHITE HART HOTEL*

The White Hart Hotel is one of half a dozen inns situated in Cricklade's main street.

The White Hart has been in Cricklade since the 1700s. It was at that time that the town's famous market originated, and the old inn must have witnessed some colourful scenes. Beasts were brought from all the surrounding counties for the fat-stock show. Picture the crowded stagecoaches winding their precarious ways through every kind of livestock and sideshow to the stable doors of the White Hart. The market ceased in the late 1700s. It was resurrected in 1837, but, sadly, it was finally abandoned in 1953.

Inside the White Hart, the customer feels obliged to poke about and study the pictures and portraits, not to mention the film stills, that adorn every nook and cranny. On one wall John Wayne is surrounded by a collection of Colt revolvers and shotguns. This legend of the westerns is reputed to have frequented the bar here. As one approaches the bar, several wise sayings catch and captivate the eye. One, 'A smile can be seen by the deaf and heard by the blind', might be judged a trifle trite in another situation. Here it seems to be well suited.

Back in the 1700s, when the White Hart was a popular staging inn, the landlord's daughter fell in love with a lowly ostler. When mine host got wind of the affair, he showed the ostler the business end of his boot and locked his daughter in her room. There she died of a broken heart. So, of course, we have a resident ghost, a weeping young lady in one of the bedrooms. She has not been seen for a decade.

LECHLADE: *THE TROUT*

The Trout lies a little way out of town. It is about a mile east of Lechlade on the A417 at St John's Bridge.

I first visited The Trout at Lechlade some forty years ago. My old Uncle Buster, who lived at Cirencester, introduced me to its pleasantly gaunt old bar. Buster always declared that it was haunted by moans and chanting, emitted from the flagstone floor. Apparently, there was an underground passage, which was yet to be discovered.

I drove down to The Trout, and was mystified when I tried to find the entrance to the car park. I was over St John's Bridge and on the wrong side of the river before I knew it. I went back across the bridge and found a parking area up a narrow lane.

What a perfect setting this ancient, lichen-covered, greystone-walled hostelry enjoys, right on the banks of the young Thames. Its sitting-out area is a must on a summer's day.

I walked round to the front of The Trout and enjoyed the fascinating view of Lechlade across the fields. I was also intrigued by a nearly modern barstool that proudly announced that it was a ducking stool dated 1850. This suggested that the landlord had a sense of humour. His customers would also need a similarly jovial disposition when visiting the outside toilet on a cold day.

It is obvious that this is a fisherman's pub. Vast river trophies in large cases adorn the walls. Advertisements for angling competitions are displayed on noticeboards. My memory served me well concerning the low-beamed ceiling and the flagstones on the floor. I enquired of the busy lady chef about the history of the inn. She handed me a menu that bore a précis of its past on the cover.

In 1220 the wooden bridge that crossed the Thames was replaced by a stone one. At the same time a hospital or almshouse was constructed by Peter Fitzherbert, and dedicated to St John the Baptist. In 1472 the main priory was dissolved by Edward

IV, but the almshouse continued as an inn, known as Ye Sygne of St John the Baptist's Head. The name was changed to The Trout in 1704. Apparently, the ancient fishery rights granted by the Royal Charter of Brethren remained, and still do to this day.

Back in Lechlade, I made a long and extensive research concerning the inn. I was told a strange story, a story that I have since authenticated. In the mid-1970s the owner of The Trout decided to turn the flagstones to save them wearing out – not an unusual operation, as it is recommended this is done every couple of hundred years, During the operation a host of skeletons was unearthed. Local records showed that in all probability they belonged to plague victims who had been interred in a mass grave. This would make sense when one considers the ecclesiastical background of The Trout. Perhaps the digging allowed the unrequited souls to escape. It may also account for the landlord's lack of knowledge about my Uncle Buster's accounts of ghostly moanings and chanting.

LECHLADE: *THE RIVERSIDE*

The Riverside is easy to find. It is a short walk from Lechlade's main street, the
A417. There is a signpost pointing to the river.

The date of The Riverside is unknown, and sadly little can be gleaned about what
is likely to be an interesting history. Legend has it that this inn was once on a
wharf where coal was delivered for the local towns. Lechlade was about as far up the
river as the big old barges could go.

Lechlade itself is a mecca for antique hunters, and it would seem that many arrive
by boat. The Riverside in summer is a pleasant scene, with the colourful boats
bobbing on the water. After a visit to the nearby antique arcade, nothing is more
welcome than a pint, and possibly a meal, here. Incidentally, a poster announces
that there is a choice of two dinners – Take it or Leave it. This is an example of the
landlord's sense of humour, as is a cardboard cut-out of a massive chef wielding a
hatchet. Statuettes of The Blues Brothers are also noticeable.

I took the photograph from the nearby bridge, which provides a viewpoint of one
of the most charming scenes on the river. Back in the bar, there is a picture of the
bridge with a dozen or so Lechlade ladies diving from it. From the modest one-piece
swimming suits it can be judged to date from the early part of the twentieth century.
Nearby is a picture taken in the early 1960s, showing people walking on the frozen
river. It is not always summer on the Thames.

There is a rumour that the whole area is to be redeveloped, which would be sad
indeed.

NEWBRIDGE: *ROSE REVIVED*

The hamlet of Newbridge stands on the A415 Abingdon-to-Witney road. The Rose Revived stands beside a small double bridge.

This is a romantic name for an attractive old inn set on a pretty, if traffic-defying, old bridge. The Rose Revived is a well-known and popular old pub. It probably dates from around 1700, but may be a good deal older. As is the case with much of the land and property in these parts, it belonged to the Harcourt Manor Estate, but became independent in the 1920s. It stands on the Thames near to where the Windrush joins its big sister after the two rivers have slowly meandered their separate ways through Gloucestershire.

The Rose Revived has been considerably extended, but in the older parts the flagstones and ancient beams remain unchanged. A brief history of the old place appears on a notice attached to the walls. In 1831 the inn was, in part, a wharf owned by John Hutt, a coal merchant from Witney. He paid £25 a year for the rights. Across the meadows, Newbridge Horse Fair was held for generations. It was finally discontinued in 1900. A local celebrity was Sir Edmund Warcup of Northmoor, whose main claim to fame was that he signed the death warrant of Charles I. His sins were miraculously forgiven after the Restoration. Charles II made him Lord Chief Justice and extended his property, to include Northmoor Church. One leaves the Rose Revived with regret; there is clearly more untapped and colourful history here.

BABLOCK HYTHE: *THE FERRYMAN*

To reach The Ferryman, it is easiest to go to the village of Stanton Harcourt or Northmoor and enquire.

The hamlet of Bablock Hythe is difficult to find, but if you achieve this, do be sure to go through the village. The road becomes narrower as one travels alongside a large caravan site, and as you reach the stripling Thames The Ferryman comes into view. The inn looks relatively modern, probably the result of much alteration over the years.

There is a romantic story here. The Ferryman (once The Ferryboat) was, in the 1760s, adorned by an attractive barmaid named Betty Rudge. The beautiful Betty spent most of her time fighting off drunken admirers. It was rough on the river in those days; even the sports of cudgel-fighting and shin-kicking were intended to give maximum pain to the contestants.

Luckily for Betty, her beauty caught the eye of a young undergraduate who was fishing by the weir. On seeing Betty, he became totally infatuated – love at first sight. It was a love that was readily reciprocated. The angling undergraduate turned out to be William Flower, Viscount Ashbrook. Despite his noble birth, he married the humble barmaid, Betty Rudge, at Northmoor church in 1766. Unfortunately, the Viscount died in 1780, aged only 37. Betty died in 1808 at the age of 63. She had remarried, and she met her end as the Dowager Lady Ashbrook. The area abounds with tales of her good and selfless deeds, and the point of this simple little story is that it is possible to be thrust from rags to riches and remain benevolent to those less fortunate.

And now, a slightly more complex character. A name not heard much these days in connection with hauntings is that of Joseph Glanville (1636–80) of Lincoln College, Oxford. Glanville was the first in-depth researcher of the paranormal. In his better-known writings he defended belief in the pre-existence of souls in *Lux Orientalis* (1662) and belief in witchcraft in *Sadulismus Triumphaius* (1681). This was a man well before his time. He also researched every supernatural spirit that he heard of, visiting literally hundreds of sites. Not the least of them was the legendary spirit 'The Drummer of Tedworth'. Another legendary ghost is that of the 'Scholar Gipsy', later expounded upon by Matthew Arnold in a poem of the same name. The poem relates the story of an Oxford student who decided to join the gypsies in search of their mysterious readings of the soul.

> Who, tired of knocking at preferment's door,
> One summer-morn forsook
> His friends, and went to learn the gypsy-lore,
> And roamed the world with that wild brotherhood
> And came, as most men deemed, to little good,
> But came to Oxford and his friends no more.

I believe even a well-versed scholar such as Arnold exaggerates with the words 'roamed the world'. The ghost of the 'Scholar Gypsy' was reported for several centuries, generally within 20 miles of Oxford. Dressed in 'hat of antique shape, and cloak of grey', our academic Romany has been witnessed on occasions in Cumnor, Fifield, Godstow and Bagley. Most regularly over the centuries he has been reported at Bablock Hythe.

> For most, I know, thou lov'st retired ground!
> Thee at the ferry Oxford riders blithe,
> Returning home on summer-nights, have met
> Crossing the stripling Thames at Bablock-hithe.

Whether or not this legendary spirit exists, or even existed, is open to discussion, but it is a fine, romantic old story.

GODSTOW: *TROUT INN*

The Trout is a little difficult to find. Head north of Oxford, turn off for either Wytham or Wolvercote and follow the Godstow signs from either village.

The Trout is the epitome of Thames inns. Its surroundings are as perfect as possible, and its fare is as varied as anywhere in the country. It is old, as old as the ruined nunnery just across the river. In fact, The Trout was built as a guest house for visitors to the nunnery, long before the first of Oxford's colleges was built.

The Benedictine nunnery is now a ruin.

The Benedictine nunnery, now no more than an attractive ruin, was put to the torch by Henry VIII, but many of the stones were saved to build an extension to the inn.

The list of historical celebrities attached to The Trout is endless, but probably the most famous is Lewis Carroll. It was on a boat trip from Oxford, a mere couple of miles away, that the idea of Alice, she of Wonderland and Looking Glass fame, was first conceived. The character is based on Alice Liddell, who, with her sisters, regularly accompanied Carroll on trips up the river.

Matthew Arnold was a regular visitor to The Trout; from the terrace you can see his 'Dreaming Spires of Oxford'. However, one Thomas Hearne, a famous Oxford historian, found The Trout not at all to his liking. In 1732 he described the goings-on there: 'booths and vicious living were there and puppet-shews and rope dancing, to the debauching and corrupting of youth'.

From the nunnery comes the tale of fair Rosamund. Rosamund was the daughter of Walter De Clifford and the beloved mistress of Henry II (1133–89), who maintained her in secret at nearby Woodstock. The King's knight, Sir Thomas, was left on guard while Henry and his son were fighting in France. Queen Eleanor took the opportunity to slay Sir Thomas and force Rosamund to drink from a poisoned chalice. Rosamund was murdered in 1175 and is buried at Godstow nunnery. Her body was not left in peace. In 1191 St Hugh, visiting his diocese, insisted that the body be exhumed and buried outside the church.

There are various stories concerning fair Rosamund's body being smuggled back into the church, only to be removed again some 300 years later. Be that as it may, there is little doubt that the smiling lady who disturbs the resident peacocks as she crosses the river by the weir is the lovely, fair Rosamund.

OXFORD: *THE BEAR*

The Bear is in Alfred Street, which turns south off the High Street, not far from the town hall.

This is probably the best-known pub in Oxford, now that the Golden Cross is no longer. It would be superfluous to add to the many written histories of the old building, but it is probably necessary to mention a few of the facts reported on the back of the menu. Here is a précis.

The small building that still stands was once the ostler's house of a vast adjacent building. The original building dated back to 1242, but came into its eminence in the seventeenth century, when stagecoach travel was at its height. By the time it closed in the early nineteenth century, it had thirty bedrooms and stabling for as many horses. The tiny ostler's house survived as a separate enterprise, and was originally named the Jolly Trooper.

It is thought that the new name comes from the crest of the Earl of Warwick, the bear and ragged staff. Personally, I consider this unlikely, as nearly every Bear in the

country, of which there are some 250, was named after the cruel sport of bear-baiting that went on at the premises. It was a form of advertisement.

The 4,500 ties, pinned to virtually everything in sight, come from a custom started in the 1950s. In those days every man who produced a necktie was presented with a free pint of beer. This custom no longer exists.

As with so many Oxford pubs, the interior of The Bear is very small, and if more than a dozen people are present it is a little claustrophobic. As always, I questioned the bar staff about the inn's history. There would seem to be nothing supernatural. I was told, however, by a young lady who knew the pub well, that a previous landlord was supposed to have hanged himself in the cellar. She invited me down and explained that it was unlikely, as the room was only 5 feet high at the most. Either the landlord was a little on the short side, or the story is a load of nonsense.

OXFORD: *THE CHEQUERS*

The Chequers is easy to overlook in Oxford's High Street. Find The Mitre and The Chequers is nearly opposite.

Although The Chequers is in Oxford's High Street, it is not that easy to find. It is not often I pass a pub's entrance twice. Like many ancient pubs in the town, it has a very small frontage. Much of the building stands in a narrow alley way just off the main street. There are many such passageways leading off Oxford's central streets, for in the Middle Ages it was far cheaper to rent commercial buildings away from the main thoroughfares. The Chequers, however, is unique in the fact that the alley ends in a beer garden, rather than joining onto another street.

The beer garden still has the look of its original function as the courtyard of a tenement. In this case, the house was that of a fifteenth-century money-changer – hence the chequers sign, denoting that the house was used for that purpose. The design of such boards goes back to Roman times, when the paymasters calculated soldiers' wages on squared cloths. Part of

the old tenement was rebuilt as a tavern in 1500, and a small guide to the property states that much of the interior is unchanged. It also states that the name did not arrive until 1605, when a licence was granted to an inn at All Saints.

In the seventeenth and eighteenth centuries it was a home to exhibitions of new gadgets and to a strange mixture of animals. It is stated that it housed, among others, several camels, a raccoon and a large fish. One wonders where, in such a confined area. More wondrous still is that it was the habitation of a giant. Where on earth did he find the room? Perhaps we can get a clue from the one-page guide to the inn. I quote: 'at one time a giant was also on show, but he was in great demand in the colleges, where his huge presence graced many a table.'

Here is a grim little story to finish with. During the dissolution of the monasteries Henry VIII's agents were very active in Oxford. Priests' holes hiding Catholic priests were numerous. One major escape route was a subterranean tunnel under the High Street, between The Chequers and The Mitre (another delightful old inn). At whichever end Henry's agents appeared, the brothers fled to the other. In the end, the agents sealed both ends, which was unfortunate for the brothers who were trapped in the middle. It is said that the sound of the chanting, bewailing, praying brothers can still be heard today as they slowly starve to death.

OXFORD: *WHITE HORSE*

The White Horse is sandwiched between two parts of Blackwells, close to the Bodleian Library and The Sheldonian in Broad Street.

Most of Oxford's favourite pubs are small, and sandwiched between larger adjacent properties. The White Horse is no exception, with Blackwell's bookshop either side of it. Apparently the inn has rejoiced in many names since its birth in the 1590s. Originally the White Mermaid, it was later the Jolly Volunteer, The Elephant after the Restoration in the 1660s and, a hundred years later, the present White Horse.

The interior is dark – romantically shaded might be a better way of describing it. It is also cosy, rather than small. The wood panelling and weathered seating create their own ambience. During building work in 1951 a painted wall was discovered and a witch's broomstick was found in the roof. I was a little uncertain of how the discoverers decided it had belonged to a witch, for so far as I know there was no pointed hat alongside it. Nearly every household owned a couple of besoms in the old days; my great-grandfather constructed thousands of them.

Along with various other establishments in Oxford, the White Horse has associations with Inspector Morse, as some of the episodes were filmed here. It was also the favourite of Bill Clinton in his university days. Finally, Sir Winston Churchill drank here on many occasions after travelling in from Blenheim, in nearby Woodstock.

OXFORD: *EAGLE AND CHILD*

St Giles is near the centre of Oxford. It meets Beaumont Street by the Ashmolean Museum. The Eagle and Child is a short walk from there.

Oxford has a great many inns. High on my list for a visit was the Eagle and Child. It is a smallish pub of great antiquity, and has been the favourite of many academics over the years.

Here follows a little of the history of this venue for academic discussion, not to say colourful argument. The name (it is known locally as the Bird and Baby) comes from the crest of the Earls of Derby, and the board depicts an eagle carrying a child. It has been an inn since 1650, when it acted as a payhouse for the Royalist troops of Charles I, who lived in Christchurch from 1642 to 1646.

The Eagle and Child was frequented by Anthony Wood, the famous diarist and antiquarian. One of Wood's claims to fame was that he had recorded, and presumably visited, all 378 alehouses in the town. Later literary regulars included J.R.R. Tolkien and

C.S. Lewis, of *Lord of the Rings* and *The Chronicles of Narnia* fame respectively. These two, with other writers and poets, named themselves 'The Inklings' and often drank and argued until the early hours in a small room that became known as the Rabbit Room.

The Eagle and Child was even smaller in those days, and comprised just two rooms – in which case Tolkien and co. must have occupied 50 per cent of the inn's area. Some time later, the pony yard was covered in and extended, to increase the area of the bar. The lack of space, and the popularity of the venue, leave little room to manoeuvre. I did, however, manage to get a photograph of a statuette of an academic Pan, complete with mortar-board and gown.

ABINGDON: *CROWN AND THISTLE*

The A415 for Abingdon turns off the A4014. The Crown and Thistle is near the Thames Bridge.

When Henry VIII dissolved the monasteries in 1538, Abingdon Abbey was no exception. However, Henry did leave the Abbey brewery, which stood directly behind the site of the Crown and Thistle. The Crown and Thistle was reputedly built in 1605, a fact not lost on me when I called exactly 400 years later.

One of the earliest records indicates that the Crown and Thistle was rented by the Cheyney family in 1624. In the seventeenth century the inn seems to have been the first among equals in a town brimming with pubs. Its main rivals appear to have been the White Hart, the New Inn and the Lamb. Only the Crown and Thistle stands intact, the others having either sunk into obscurity or been altered out of all recognition.

In the late 1700s the Crown and Thistle was the home of landlord James Powell. Powell, a man of vision, brought many and various types of entertainment to the inn. Apart from the cock-fighting and wrestling matches that seemed to be weekly occurrences, all types of betting and gambling took place, reaching a climax during the famous Abingdon races.

Powell appealed to the more affluent and esteemed among the local populace. He provided services as well as good ale, food and shelter. Samuel Crawcouer, a German from Hanover, had a room here where he ran a business of dentistry and operations on teeth and gums. From the same premises Mr Sutton, or Gamble, advertised the new and rather unreliable inoculation against smallpox. Chevalier Taylor, an oculist, advertised eye-glasses and claimed nearly all of the crowned heads of Europe as his patients.

In 1773 Powell played host to John Elwes of Marcham, who was the prospective parliamentary candidate for Berkshire. Powell's inventiveness led to his success when the first mail coaches arrived. In 1784 he became a postmaster, which led to his turning down the position of Mayor of Abingdon because he was too busy. Another string to his entrepreneurial bow was his marriage to Miss Catherine Taylor of the Kingston Inn. She was described as being of genteel fortune and good looks. How could Powell go wrong? He didn't.

I called at the Crown and Thistle just as the landlord was preparing to celebrate its 400 years of existence. I enjoyed a pint, and the landlord found time to show me around this beautiful old inn. When we returned to the bar I put my inevitable question.

'Have you any resident ghosts?' I asked.

'How many do you want?' he said.

'How many have you got?' I replied.

'Well, at least four resident ones and a couple that drop in occasionally,' came his answer.

The landlord then went on to relate the many incidents at the inn, but those are stories for another day, and readers are also recommended Jacqueline Smith and John Carter's excellent book, *Inns and Alehouses of Abingdon*.

ABINGDON: *BROAD FACE*

The Broad Face is very near the bridge in Bridge Street, close to the Crown and Thistle.

Most of the other ancient inns in Abingdon with a story to tell have ceased to exist. At the seven or eight ancient ones that remain, neither manager nor bar staff could throw any light on their histories. So I tried the Broad Face because of its unique name. It is a tidy and well-situated inn on the corner of Bridge Street and Thames Street. Of the facts that it faces the Thames and, as with several others, is a dropping-off place for river goods, there is little to tell.

So what of the name? Some fanciful stories exist. One is that the inn derived its name from the swollen corpses that were frequently pulled from the river here, and that the inn was the scene of autopsies. Only slightly less macabre is the suggestion that the name came from the bodies of men hanged at the nearby Abingdon gaol. But, as the inn and name predate the gaol by a few decades, this seems unlikely.

A slightly more likely, but less exciting, explanation (and the one put forward in *Inns and Alehouses of Abingdon*) is that the Broad Face was once called the Saracen's Head, and that the sign was much overpainted, eventually leaving only the facial features.

For myself, I believe that the name comes from the inn's unique position on two streets and its virtually curved exterior. Although quite small, it was two faced, or

broad faced. It is not often that I go for the mundane explanation, but in this case it is the one that I favour. Incidentally, when I used to drive great lorries over Abingdon Bridge, the Broad Face had a massive smiling face painted on and overlapping two walls. Ostentatious in the extreme, yes, but also noticeable, which was surely the idea.

DORCHESTER: *GEORGE HOTEL*

The A4074 Henley-to-Oxford road bypasses Dorchester, but it is clearly signposted. The George is opposite the gatehouse of the ruined abbey, in the High Street.

Dorchester was once a city blessed with a cathedral, an abbey, a monastery and at least seven churches. It was described in some detail by the Venerable Bede. There were, however, an Iron Age settlement and a Roman hill fort at Dorchester long before any of these buildings.

Opposite the gatehouse of the Norman abbey, all that is left of the town's former glory, stands the George Hotel. It is thought to stand on the site of the priory hospice, which dated back to 1140. The present inn is a mere youth, dating only to 1450. An external view of the building shows a half-timbered and tiled structure. The galleries and the travellers' lodges are among the few remaining in the country,

and are reached by a staircase from the courtyard. The bar is snug rather than small, but the medieval dining hall is something to behold. Here, ancient beams and timbers soar into the roof, and ancient chimneys sweep out of sight and disappear among the rafters. The entire aspect of The George is romantically magnificent, and it has been described as 'the finest example of medieval domestic architecture in the land'.

The George Hotel really came into its own as a coaching inn. Among a list of famous personages who stayed there over the years is Sarah Churchill, the first Duchess of Marlborough. Apparently, coach drivers would plan to arrive here at sundown so that their famous passenger could spend the night at her favourite inn before continuing to Blenheim Palace the next morning.

There is a rather strange little story attached to The George at Dorchester, but I should mention that I have heard a very similar tale about the George Hotel at Wallingford and The Bull at Wargave.

The tale goes that the daughter of the landlord of the time fell in love with a local coachman. Believing that a lowly coachman was not fit to marry his daughter, the landlord devised his downfall, and the young man was murdered. When she heard the news, the young lady became insane with grief and had to be incarcerated – in the Vicar's Room.

WALLINGFORD: *GEORGE HOTEL*

Follow the A329 to Wallingford. The George Hotel is in the High Street and is very easy to find.

One could write a complete book on the history of Wallingford. The town has a very colourful past indeed.

King Alfred fought off the Danes in 871, but they returned a century later and set fire to the town. Parts of the old rampart and ditch are said to be still discernible. The castle, of which very little remains and that private property, was the location for the signing of the treaty between Stephen and Matilda that ended England's first civil war. Henry II held parliament here, the Black Prince resided here, Henry VIII was a frequent visitor, Elizabeth I summered here and Charles I held the town during the Civil War. The castle also has associations with King John, Richard II and John of Gaunt. It was destroyed by Parliamentarians in 1652.

In 1349 only forty-four households were left after the Black Death had invaded, and in 1537 a man was placed in the pillory after first having had his ears cut off for spreading the rumour that Henry VIII was dead.

In 1836 Wallingford was plagued by beggars. Special marshals, complete with rattles, blunderbusses and truncheons, were installed to keep order.

That about sums up the history of Wallingford.

And now – to the George Hotel. It was around during much of the above history, but the date of its origin is debatable. Some historians place it as early as 1550, but, as in good pub tradition, nothing is recorded until a murder took place there in 1626. The George is a prominent building on the High Street. It looks every inch a coaching inn, and was probably adopted for that purpose.

Inside it has been tastefully modernised, and at my last visit the massive open fireplace remained. I did a BBC radio programme here in the 1980s and was told there is a blocked-off underground passage here. I was also told that Dick Turpin had a regular room here, information that I received with scepticism.

The George at Wallingford has a similar story to that of The George at Dorchester, but it differs in a few details. In this version the daughter of a former landlord became infatuated with a handsome and wealthy young man of the town. The couple were to be married, and had the best of prospects. One evening, as the man was entering the house that he had built as a surprise for his future bride, he was bludgeoned to death by burglars. Hearing the news, the landlord's daughter grieved herself into insanity and had to be locked away in her bedroom to prevent her from committing suicide. She spent the remainder of her days painting weird murals with her fingers, her only materials being tears and soot. Naturally, after her death the room became known as the Teardrop Room, and, just as naturally, her ghost is occasionally heard bewailing her lost love.

With two inns bearing the same name, being of similar appearance and being geographically close to one another, a story can become a trifle involved. You pay your money and you take your choice of location.

MOULSFORD: *BEETLE AND WEDGE*

From Goring follow the B4009 or the A329 to Moulsford. The Beetle and Wedge is signposted from the village.

To the casual visitor there would seem very little to Moulsford other than the Beetle and Wedge. But the village boasts two private schools, a nursing home, a seventeenth-century manor and a fine little church, restored by Gilbert Scott in 1847.

Moulsford is also truly proud of its railway bridge, one of seven that cross the Thames between London and Oxford. Brunel lovingly constructed this fine bridge, which crosses the river on four beautiful, architecturally harmonised brick arches.

After Dorchester the river widens dramatically and becomes far more grandiose. Snug beside the riverside lies the Beetle and Wedge. Here the Thames Walk gives one a choice of taking the north bank route or the south bank route to Wallingford.

The inn dates back to the seventeenth century, but has been tastefully altered on several occasions. Incidentally, a beetle was a long, heavy-headed mallet, and of course we all know what a wedge is.

Today the Beetle has an ambience of warmth and efficiency without the snobbish attitude that often accompanies such feelings. The hotel's brochure advertises lunch in the garden, an elegant dinner in the dining room and a hearty meal or a drink in the boathouse. What could be more English?

I chose a pint of traditional ale from the boathouse and absconded to the water garden. The glittering Thames was splendid, recalling the atmosphere evoked by Jerome K. Jerome, who wrote much of *Three Men in a Boat* here.

There was, however, another author who took a fancy to the Beetle and Wedge. H.G. Wells, who invented the *Invisible Man* and saw well into the future in *The War of the Worlds*, stayed here while writing the slightly more modest but equally satisfying *The History of Mr Polly*.

STREATLEY: *THE BULL*

*The Bull stands beside the A329 directly opposite the B4009 turning
to Goring.*

This is another quaint old pub, and has been for over 500 years. In 1833 George King was being taken from Wantage to Reading to stand trial for murder. King, a part-time bean-cutter, had slaughtered his landlady at Wantage's White Hart by decapitating her with his bean-hook. It was the most horrendous of crimes, and all for the few shillings in the landlady's purse. Incidentally, the poor woman's surviving relatives were not above making a small profit by showing her separated head and body to anybody ghoulish enough to pay a small entrance fee. A full report on the heinous murder and trial can be found in *I'll Be Hanged*.

Although the evidence against King was overwhelming, he stubbornly refused to confess. However, when the constables stopped for refreshments at The Bull, the young bean-cutter suddenly noticed a picture of a middle-aged woman hanging in the bar. The picture had a vague likeness to Anne Pullin, the unfortunate landlady. King took this as an omen.

'It's her, Mrs Pullin,' screamed King. 'She's following me. I'll kill her again.'

The constables held the young farmhand as he flung himself against the picture. Moments later, King was stuttering out a confession before a surprised landlord and his customers.

The supernatural appearances at The Bull have absolutely nothing to do with the distraught young murderer. They are far older and more distinct. The story, however, is quite a romantic one.

The legend relates that in the early 1500s a monk had secret assignations with a novice at a nearby nunnery. The Bull was the chosen venue for these covert meetings, which were as passionate as they were short-lived. Discovered, the pair were slain on the spot and buried beneath two massive yew trees in the garden. For years it was rumoured that on balmy nights the spiritual lovers forsook their lonely graves and walked hand in hand in the garden.

But the infatuated couple have not been witnessed for some years – if indeed they ever were.

GORING: *MILLER OF MANSFIELD*

From Pangbourne follow the A329 towards Oxford. On entering Streatley, turn right at The Bull (B4009). Cross the river and the Miller of Mansfield is directly opposite.

This is a large, intriguing inn set at the centre of Goring village, opposite the church and just a little way from the Thames. The story of the board is a little vague. The most I can glean is that a miller, apparently from Mansfield, got up to some jiggery-pokery with an unnamed king. Whatever his little scam, it was discovered by the royal personage, who forgave him so long as he built an inn on the site. This the miller did, and some sort of hostelry has been here ever since. An old sign once showed a jovial king lifting his glass and saying to the miller, 'Here goode fellow, I'll drink to thee.'

The building is probably seventeenth century, which implies that it, or a predecessor on the site, was witness to the Goring disaster in 1674. Before the bridge was built in the 1830s, the only way across the Thames was by ferry. After a great feast day an overloaded boat, with approximately a hundred people on board, was heading from Goring to Streatley. Celebrating crowds waited on both banks. A report in the Oxford and London papers states that the ferryman was 'imprudently rowing too near the lock'.

The very scarce reports state that at the last minute the ferryman tried vainly to pull away, but it was too late and the ferry overturned, emptying its human cargo into the river. Between fifty and sixty men, women and children were drowned. This disaster was a bone of contention between the two villages for well over a century.

PANGBOURNE: *THE SWAN*

From Pangbourne High Street turn right into Station Road (A329). This becomes Shooter's Hill. The Swan is directly on the right.

Pangbourne is one of the best-loved and most picturesque parts of the Thames. It is the sparkling Thames, the friendly Thames; the Thames inhabited and loved by Toad, Mole and Ratty.

From the Ridgeway down, one sees conglomerations of different periods of architecture. For some unknown reason, some attractive houses on the waterfront were nicknamed the Seven Deadly Sins.

This is farming country, proud of its livestock. In 1797 a Tidmarsh farm hog weighed 40 score pounds and had 11 inches of fat on its shoulders.

The Swan occupies one of the most attractive sites on the river. It appears splendidly, as appealing as unexpected, on a bend in the Oxford Road. The waterside bar is magnificent. It is a pleasure indeed to drink here, with the sound of the weir chanting its endless refrain in the background. It was this ambience that made The Swan so attractive to Jerome K. Jerome, who featured it in *Three Men in a Boat*. H.G. Wells strolled here while contemplating *The History of Mr Polly*.

Although it is a magnet for many of our authors, the one most associated with Pangbourne in general, and with The Swan in particular, is Kenneth Grahame. Grahame lived in the village for many years, after moving from nearby Blewbury. Church Cottage, older than time, with its massive ship's bell at the front door, was his home. It is known that The Swan enjoyed the author's regular patronage. Grahame had already established his popularity through books such as *The Golden Age*, *Dream Days* and *The Wind in the Willows* before moving to Pangbourne. In fact, his most famous story is reputed to have been compiled from letters that he had written to his son in serial form. Fortunately, the letters had been collected by the boy's governess, and the author later turned them into book form at Cookham Dean in 1908.

Sadly, Grahame's son died in an accident at Oxford University. The great children's author never recovered and wrote no more. He joined his son in his grave in 1920.

On entering The Swan recently, I learned two further facts, printed on the wall. One is that The Swan was previously a grain store, where barges pulled up to be loaded. The other was that it once lay partially in two counties, Berkshire and Oxfordshire. It had to apply to two licensing authorities and its separate bars had different closing times, thereby causing regulars to change bars for an extra half an hour of imbibing.

Another tale is told, which I find a trifle suspect. The Swan stands on Shooter's Hill, which is said to derive its name from posses chasing highwaymen. Apparently, if a felon could reach the other side of the Thames, he would then in be Oxfordshire and be safe. It is suggested that Shooter's Hill was where the pursuing party let off its firearms to impede such a venture. Less exciting, but probably closer to the truth, is that local country gentlemen gathered here on Sundays to have their 'sport', shooting birds from the sky and later retiring to church with a loud chorus of 'All Things Bright and Beautiful'.

PANGBOURNE: *CROSS KEYS*

Enter Pangbourne by the 329 Reading–Oxford road. Enter the High Street and turn sharp left into Church Street (A340). The Cross Keys is immediately on the left.

There are at least three other very well-known inns in this most pleasant of villages. I plumped for the Cross Keys because it was slightly less well known than some of the others. As I have frequently experienced in the cases of other serenely attractive inns, no one knows anything about the building's history.

The date of the building's origin is unknown, but parts of the structure are definitely very old. In the absence of any history, I can but describe the Cross Keys.

It has been much altered inside, but many of the beams remain, their positions possibly having been changed over the years. On the walls are pictures of balloons –

the people-carrying kind – polo scenes and a great collage of photos of the heads of locals in fancy dress. For some unknown reason there is a tombstone in one corner of the restaurant. Outside is a well-stocked, flowery beer garden that enhances the nearly perfect riverside setting. This is the Pang, which joins the Thames some hundred yards away. On the patio is a flower-strewn, wooden-sided, canvas-topped, permanent marquee. As I talked briefly to a bearded gentleman in a straw boater we could have jumped straight out of Monet's Boating Party. Among others, there is a nice little work of Yeats on one particular beam:

> Wine comes in at the mouth
> And love comes in at the eye;
> That's all we shall know for truth
> Before we grow old and die.
> I lift the glass to my mouth,
> I look at you, and I sigh

More arresting is a shorter message along a beam: 'When you have lost your inns, drown your empty selves. For you have lost the last of England.' This close to the Thames, this is a little too appropriate, especially considering the closure rate of our pubs.

TILEHURST: *THE ROEBUCK*

Take the Oxford Road out of Reading (A329), travel several miles through Tilehurst towards Purley. Have patience: The Roebuck will appear on the left.

This is a good, staunch, plain old pub, verging on the gaunt, but not unattractive. The A4 is busy here in the direction from Pangbourne, and it can be easy to miss even such a large building as this.

The Roebuck is a pub-man's pub, and has provided sustenance and shelter for a couple of hundred years. The name, a good, old-fashioned one that was adequate for many years, was changed to the Beethoven in the 1990s in an attempt to turn it into a theme pub. During those days I did a programme here for the BBC. I had to bite my tongue to prevent myself saying 'Brahms and Liszt'.

For many years The Roebuck enjoyed the patronage of 'The Admiral', a retired naval gentleman who lived nearby. The Admiral (a rank suggested but never verified) still looked upon himself as a protector of this blessed isle and patrolled the hills,

complete with telescope, scanning for invaders coming up the Thames from London. It was his intention to be the first to warn the local populace – notwithstanding the logic that invaders who had got as far as Reading would have already conquered the capital, and the unwelcome news would not have been in short supply.

The date of The Admiral's demise is unknown, but rumour has it that he died in suspicious circumstances. I have tried in vain to uncover the facts of his death, but have been unable even to trace his name.

My visit in the 1990s was occasioned by reports of poltergeist activity at the pub. A former landlord had claimed that heavy furniture had moved without making any noise and that locked doors and windows sprang open. Heavy footsteps had been heard in the corridors and on the gravel outside. The old boy himself, complete with hat and spyglass, had been seen standing level with one of the upstairs windows on no fewer than three occasions, and dogs disliked certain rooms at certain times.

Nothing untoward has happened at The Roebuck and The Admiral seems a benign old chap. I hope he is comfy, and long may he remain so. After all, he adds a little character.

READING: *THE SUN*

The Sun is in Castle Street, near St Mary's Butts in the centre of Reading.

Considering The Sun's eventful, not to say chequered, history, it may not be surprising to learn that the old inn has experienced strange, supernatural encounters – some unexplained gurgling noises, coming from under the floor, described in the 1960s as mysterious chantings.

The history of the old building is worth a few words. There is thought to have been a hostelry of sorts on the site since the thirteenth century. It is also rumoured that an underground passage leading to the ruins of Reading Abbey still exists. The rumour is in all probability true, as doorways and archways, now bricked up, have been found in the floor of the building. We know for certain that there is a large, bricked-up hall under The Sun and that, in the heyday of coaching in the early eighteenth century, more than fifty horses were stabled there. There is also reputed to be another subterranean tunnel, leading to the ostler's house across the street. This tunnel is said to have been used by French prisoners from the Napoleonic wars, who were interned here. They used it in an unsuccessful attempt at escape. As late as 1920 a Norman archway was discovered during renovations, and a small cell was also exposed. In 1948 the subterranean hall collapsed completely, shortly after a visit from the Mayor of Reading. Many circus elephants stabled here at the time by Bertram Mills were not so fortunate. Apparently, they found their confined quarters unsuitable and caused their own demise by pulling on the supporting posts and beams, thereby causing the collapse of the hall.

For an even sadder and a rather unlikely tale about The Sun we must go back to the thirteenth-century hostelry on this site, which was demolished centuries ago. Legend has it that a monk from Reading Abbey fell in love with a local beauty. Forgoing, or temporarily forgetting, his vows, he made clandestine visits to the lady (no doubt finding the underground passageway a convenience). Unfortunately, the young beauty's gaze fell upon a handsome young soldier who frequented the inn. The monk found out and was heartbroken. The soldier turned out to be fickle and promiscuous, and informed the besotted lady that he would shortly be leaving with his regiment and another woman. In a fit of depression the distressed damsel flung herself into the River Thames and drowned.

Ten years later, while passing the hostelry, the same monk noticed the same soldier, well in his cups and boasting to friends of his many sexual conquests. In a jealous rage the monk grabbed the soldier and throttled the life out of him. Before he expired, the soldier managed to pull a knife from his belt and fatally stab the monk in the throat.

A cheerful little tale.

READING: *GEORGE HOTEL*

The George Hotel is situated on the corner of King Street and Minster Street, near the eastern end of Broad Street in the centre of Reading.

A somewhat Herculean stone's throw from the river stands the George Hotel. Gone are the days when every other building in Berkshire's capital was an ancient coaching inn. After the courageous passengers had braved the dangers of Maidenhead Thicket, the town's countless inns were a welcome sight. Reading was a

natural overnight stop for coaches journeying between the capital and Bristol, Bath or Plymouth. For many years an ancient coach stood in the courtyard of The George, and its turning circle can still be seen. The coaches entered via King Street, and the passengers would alight, looking forward to a night between The George's famous lavender-scented sheets. The coach would then proceed to Minster Street, where the horses were stabled for the night.

In 1812 William Darter, a journalist, reported how a Mr Moody, a coach proprietor, would buy two baskets of bad eggs from a Mr Millard. He would then supply them to his passengers so that they could walk down to the market and pelt some unfortunate fellow in the pillory. Not to be outdone, the cook at The George would supply refuse from his slaughterhouse for the same purpose. This additional entertainment made The George particularly popular with travellers, giving them something to chuckle over when they continued their journey.

The George reputedly has two ghosts, a maid and a butler. Both, however, are rather unsuited to such a prestigious venue. Sightings of either of them are very rare.

CAVERSHAM: *CROWN ON THE BRIDGE*

*As the name implies, the Crown on the Bridge nestles next to Caversham
Bridge on the northern side of the river.*

This is a nice, friendly little pub, right on the waterfront. But the Crown on the
Bridge has a gruesome association.

It was reputedly outside The Crown that a police tent was pitched when three tiny
bodies were pulled from the Thames. Another small cadaver was found in the
Kennet, and two others were found when police dragged nearby Clappers Pool. The
year was 1896, and these events shocked the people of Reading, as Londoners had
been shocked the previous year by a similar large number of bodies. Each of the
Reading babies had been strangled with a red tape, to one end of which was attached
a brick.

The Crown was a favourite pub of Mrs Stanfield. Fat and jovial, she enjoyed a
drink there with her family – her robust daughter, Polly, and her son-in-law, Arthur
Palmer. They were sometimes accompanied by two pasty young children. Thought to
be relatives, the two youngsters, both under 9 years old, were later discovered to be
Elle Oliver, a girl who had arrived from Plymouth, and a boy named Willie Thornton.

The first body was discovered purely by accident. A bargee pulled up his pole and
found a small package on the end. A tiny arm poked out. It was wrapped in three
pieces of brown paper, the innermost of which was addressed to a Mrs Dyer
of Kensington Road, Reading. The police called at the address, but the
bird had flown – fortunately only as far as Caversham.

Mrs Dyer, alias Mrs Stanfield and Mrs Thomas among others, was soon
arrested. The police found cupboards full of baby clothes, bills for advertisements
in London and provincial newspapers and, saddest of all, many telegrams
and letters from frightened and worried mothers who had paid to leave their children
in the care of this seemingly kind, benign and devout old lady.

The outcome of the trial was a foregone conclusion. Mrs Stanfield

Mrs Dyer's house in Reading.

was charged with the murder of tiny Doris Marmon from Cheltenham – whose mother, Evalina, made a very sad, weeping spectacle in court – and with that of a small boy named Symons, whose parents could not be found. Evidence was extremely strong and included a confession penned by Mrs Dyer in Reading gaol. The 'baby farmer' pleaded guilty, but insane. The jury would have none of it. She was hanged at Newgate in June 1896. The biggest concern of Billington, the hangman, was how to dispatch the 16-stone woman without pulling her head off. He accomplished this by fixing her arms with ropes so that they absorbed some of the shock.

This vile Victorian woman was dispatched in one piece.

CAVERSHAM: *THE GRIFFIN*

After crossing Caversham Bridge from Reading, turn left into Church Road.
The Griffin lies directly on the left.

Caversham is joined to Reading by two bridges. For many years there have been calls for a third to ease the traffic congestion.

On the now-vanished thirteenth-century wooden bridge, the Royalists were put to rout by the Roundheads, following a valiant attempt to save Caversham. Even earlier,

on what is now known as De Montfort Island, Robert De Montfort fought a duel with Henry De Essex in the presence of Henry II. Essex had been accused of cowardice for throwing down the Royal Standard at a battle in Wales. De Montfort won the contest, and Essex nearly died of his wounds before being escorted to Reading Abbey, where he later joined the brotherhood.

Sadly, the original old Griffin was demolished in 1911 and the present one was built. This in no way detracts from the charm of the later inn. At its rear, lush green lawns sweep down to the sparkling Thames.

In 1723 the original Griffin was the last known call of a farmer named Jonathan Blagrave. Blagrave was on his way home to his farm at Upper Caversham after a successful day at Reading market. This good-natured man was generous to a fault, and every customer was treated to a drink and a story of Blagrave's astute business ability.

Sadly for the jovial farmer, three young people in the other, smaller bar heard his boastings. All three, two young men and a young woman, were down on their luck and were looking for a solution to their financial difficulties.

Blagrave left The Griffin at three o'clock on Sunday morning, and, as he plodded his way up Caversham Hill, he was set upon by three footpads, his skull was cracked and his purse was stolen. Although dying, he managed to crawl to The Roebuck and raise the alarm. He died an hour later.

At the time the fledgling *Reading Mercury* reported that 'three young people were took up on suspicion'. In a later edition it was reported that Ambrose Strange, who had killed Blagrave, was to be hanged in chains at Tyler's Heath. There was no mention at that time of the other two miscreants.

In 1888, some 165 years after the affair, workmen digging in Woodcote Road discovered three skeletons, two male and one female. They had been stretched, which is consistent with having been hanged in chains.

SONNING: *THE BULL*

The Bull is in the centre of Sonning opposite the church.

The Bull stands in the ancient and expensive village of Sonning. The twin bridges over the Thames here separate the luxurious Old House Hotel and the equally resplendent French Horn Hotel. Sonning is probably a little too chocolate-box in style

for me; everything is just a bit too perfect. As is the case with many villages, it is reputed to have associations with Dick Turpin. Legend suggests that the highwayman's aunt lived here, at the Dog Inn. When Dick was being pursued one night, he dropped his horse off at his aunt's subterranean stables and somehow crossed the river on foot. I have ascertained that indeed there was once a pub called the Dog at Sonning, but the rest of the story I believe to be pure fantasy. I wonder whether the stagecoach he robbed turned back into a pumpkin.

The Bull is probably late fourteenth or early fifteenth century. It is adjacent to the church, and the churchyard once formed part of The Bull's courtyard.

The old inn is reputed to have been a hostelry for pilgrims who came to be blessed by St Sarlic, Sarlic being a corruption of Sigeric, the then Saxon Bishop of Sonning. The Bull was also a regular haunt of the Bishop of Salisbury. On the joyful occasions of his visits a sumptuous meal was prepared, and the wine flowed copiously for several days.

The Bull has changed little over the centuries, the original rambling white walls and exterior timbers still stand, as do the open fires and massive beams.

The old hostelry is an archetypal example of serenity, standing between the church and the flowing Thames. But wait one minute. In 1914 there was one devil of a melée and kerfuffle when police tried to interview and arrest a group of suffragettes who, they thought, were responsible for setting alight the nearby Wargrave church. And The Bull was hardly all sweet serenity and light some seventy-five years earlier, in 1838, when workers employed by Isambard Kingdom Brunel started a violent demonstration after a meeting at The Bull. Eventually, the village constable quelled the riotous behaviour. Talking later, at a meeting at which he was commended for his stolid bravery, Constable Charles Flower stated that it had been no easy matter, and that he and the local blacksmith had broken four staves in bringing the workers to order.

However, after that couple of hiccups the old inn is once again a cornerstone of tranquillity.

WARGRAVE: *WHITE HART*

The White Hart is in the centre of this village, in the High Street, which is part of the Henley Road (A321).

The White Hart at Wargrave is one of four ancient inns in the High Street of this charming village.

The front has been spruced up recently, the name emblazoned on the wall in a jazzed-up type of lettering. I am sorry to say that the ancient pump-handled petrol pumps have disappeared. Inside, the White Hart is functional rather than elegant. It is a hotel, but mostly a pub – which is scarce enough these days.

If you study the inn board here, it is possible to detect that this particular White Hart has a collar, in fact a golden collar, and thereby hangs a tale.

The legend goes that a magnificent specimen of hart gave the king (which one is unknown) an exhausting and adventurous chase through Windsor Forest. Eventually the animal was cornered by the river, in the vicinity of what is now called Wargrave. The monarch refused to have such a noble and courageous beast slain. Taking a gold chain from around his own neck, he placed it around that of the hart, his intention being that the collar would be instantly recognisable and the beast would not be hunted – by royal decree.

Before we leave Wargrave, I must mention Richard, 7th Earl of Barrymore. The White Hart is old enough to remember the local lad's rakish exploits, not the least of which was a regular charge on horseback through the village, firing his revolvers at the inn signs. Although Barrymore indulged in a series of boisterous adventures, he was benevolent to Wargrave. He provided the village with a theatre, built next to Barrymore House beside the Thames. Unfortunately, the demonic gambler regularly ran out of funds. He was forced to join the Berkshire militia in the early 1790s to escape his debtors. One day, while Barrymore was escorting a party of French

prisoners, his gun went off accidentally and he was fatally wounded. This was unfortunate not only for Barrymore but also for the culture lovers of Wargrave. After his demise, Barrymore's debtors descended on the village and removed the theatre, stone by stone.

HENLEY-ON-THAMES: *RED LION HOTEL*

The Red Lion is situated next to Henley Bridge on the northern, Oxfordshire side of Henley-on-Thames.

This is one beautiful old hotel. Even the lopsided timber-framed old buildings surrounding the car park are romantic. Add to this the silver Thames and a view towards the blue and white tents of the regatta, and life is good.

I called here early in July, just after the regatta, when the town was indulging in its festival. I strolled down the long hallway passage from the car park to the bar.

Along each side were pictures of old Henley, bearded oarsmen, rowers in school caps, vintage cars, riverside scenes with ladies under parasols and overdressed in such an assemblage of clothing that they must have sweltered almost to death.

I enjoyed a pint in the snug bar, guarded by an enormous statue of the king of beasts – unfortunately grey, not red. I gleaned that the Red Lion had been receiving guests since the fifteenth century. However, little, if any, of the present building is as early as that. The Lion was best known as a coaching inn, and boasts that it has played host to three sovereigns. One was Charles I, well before coaching days, but the identities of the other two are not known. The hotel apparently has a picture of Charles I, together with his queen, Henrietta.

A less gallant guest was Captain Willie Cranstoun, the lover of Mary Blandy (see the Little Angel, Remenham), who was billeted here in the 1740s. It was at the Red Lion that they first had their clandestine rendezvous. It was also from the Red Lion that the cowardly Captain took a coach to pastures new, leaving Mary to face the music and literally 'take the drop'.

Another famous visitor to the Red Lion, somewhat after the Blandy affair, was William Shenstone, the famous eighteenth-century poet. Shenstone drank at the Red Lion in 1750 and inscribed these famous lines on one of its window panes – now, sadly, lost:

> Who'er has travelled life's dull round,
> Where'er his stages may have been,
> May sigh to think he still has found
> The warmest welcome, at an inn.

BISHAM: *BULL INN*

The Bull stands about half a mile south of Marlow Bridge. Follow signs from Marlow to Bisham.

As I have extolled the interior of the Bull Inn in several other books, I shall not elaborate on it here. A message on the wall tells us that the inn has been around for some 650 years. However, it seems that there was some type of refreshment house here even before that. The Bull was once a stopover and place of refreshment for the nearby Bisham Abbey. Among its guests have been King Henry VIII, Anne of Cleves, Queen Mary, Sir William Cecil and his son Robert Cecil (secretary to Elizabeth I). There are, of course, many other historical celebrities, both famous and infamous, but predating any of these splendid characters were the Knights Templar.

The Knights Templar were founded in Jerusalem in 1118. They were reputed to be a highly principled and moralistic society, and protected the pilgrims visiting the Holy Sepulchre in Jerusalem. The rather secretive brotherhood quickly became rich

and powerful. From their base in Jerusalem, they built colleges and schools in many lands, including an establishment for learning at Bisham. Shortly after the suppression of the Knights Templar for heresy, Bisham became an Augustinian priory. In 1537 it became a Benedictine abbey, only to be dissolved three years later. Henry VIII then gave it to Anne of Cleves as a wedding gift. In 1553 Queen Mary, a Catholic, presented it to Sir Thomas Hoby in appreciation for his plotting against her father. Sir Thomas settled there for many decades with his beautiful, if stern, wife, Elizabeth.

Elizabeth's effigy graces nearby All Saints' Church. The graceful figure belies a human tragedy. Elizabeth's life is well documented. She had four intelligent children who were a credit to her. There is also mention of William Hoby, and thereby hangs a mystery.

It was well known that Elizabeth was a strict disciplinarian, and authoritarian to an extreme – corporal punishment was the norm. William was a slow learner, and his inborn arrogance led to many confrontations. After an altercation one day, William was locked in a small room. Shortly afterwards, Elizabeth was summoned by the Queen to London (some say Windsor). She left with all due haste, unfortunately

forgetting to inform anyone of William in his tiny prison. When she returned a week or more later, she rushed frantically to the door, only to find that her son had starved to death.

This is a sad little story, which seems to be authenticated by some tear-stained schoolbooks found in 1840, with the name 'William Hoby' printed on the cover.

REMENHAM: *LITTLE ANGEL*

The Little Angel is situated approximately 100 yards from the Berkshire side of Henley Bridge, where the A321 meets the A423.

The Little Angel at Remenham is not to be confused with The Angel just over the bridge at Henley.

In the Middle Ages trade and travel in England increased. Pilgrims and merchants traversed the hazardous trackways, and people travelled in groups as a means of defence against footpads and bandits. The inns tried to encourage trade, and found that religious signs, albeit sometimes suspect to the travellers, gave confidence.

Surely they would be less likely to have their throat cut at an inn displaying a mitre, star of Bethlehem, or angel. Such boards, therefore, denote some of the oldest inns in the country.

Hence, the Little Angel at Remenham. It nestles at the foot of an extremely steep hill on the Maidenhead Road. At the top of the hill is Park Place, once the home of Frederick, Prince of Wales, the father of George III, for twenty years. A cave part-way up the hill was once the home of a latter-day hermit. He was anti-progress and could not abide motor cars. As late as 1910 the recluse would emerge from his cave and throw chunks of chalk at vehicles as they progressed tortuously up the gradient at a speed of 2 miles an hour.

Park Place and the Little Angel both had associations with the Henley spinster murderess Mary Blandy. In 1752 the 30-year-old Mary Blandy was accused of murdering her father. She had become infatuated with Captain Cranstoun (see the Red Lion Hotel, Henley). The captain was billeted in the town, but Mary's father objected to the match, and so was removed by being poisoned – probably through a scheme initiated by Cranstoun, who promptly disappeared.

Mary was placed under house arrest at her home in Hart Street, but, finding her door open one morning, she decided to take a walk over the bridge to Remenham.

Captain Cranstoun
and Miss Blandy.

She had not gone far when a mob of market customers dogged her footsteps, screaming 'murderess' and other abuse. She was struck by pieces of rotten fruit and began to panic. She fled to the Little Angel, where the landlady had been a lifelong friend. Mary knocked frantically at the door and was taken inside, and the door was barred.

Mary Blandy was later apprehended and taken into custody by the village constable, Richard Fisher. Fisher took no chances. He shackled Mary hand and foot before transporting her to Oxford Castle prison. Mary Blandy was convicted, sentenced and executed at Oxford Castle in 1752.

A play about Mary, *The Hanging Wood*, is performed regularly at Henley and in the surrounding area.

MEDMENHAM: *DOG AND BADGER*

Take the A4155 Henley-to-Marlow road. Medmenham and the Dog and Badger are midway between the two towns.

A lane opposite the Dog and Badger leads to the old ferry place from where Charles II crossed the Thames in 1678. A short walk further along the Thames path discloses the remains of St Mary's Abbey. Of the original built in 1204 very little remains, but much of the ruined folly tower constructed by the notorious Sir Francis Dashwood still stands. Dashwood turned this attractive backwater into a realm of debauchery in the mid-eighteenth century. He adopted and developed St Mary's Abbey, a short ride on horseback from his famous caves at West Wycombe. The West Wycombe tales have been adequately reported over the years, and now little remains. However, the descriptions of pornographic inscriptions, indecent religious paintings, doors in the shape of vaginas and a garden designed in the shape of a naked female body would seem historically correct.

Medmenham seems to have had less elaborate props than West Wycombe, but the orgies of debauchery and revelry were no less sexual, sensual or sinful. The 'nuns' at Medmenham seemed to occupy themselves with just as much diligence as did their sisters a little further north.

The Dog and Badger has stood beside the Henley–Marlow Road since the fourteenth century. Dashwood's brotherhood clearly used it, but apparently did not defile it. The old inn enjoyed such a respectable reputation that couples had their banns read here before they were repeated in the church. Thankfully, the old building is little changed. The outside is stone, brick and timbered. The three old dormer windows remain. Inside, there is a long, low, busy bar, which had been tastefully modified the last time I called. There are the inevitable low beams, pewters and brasses. Sadly, however, a large area is now taken up by dining tables. I realise that this is a sign of the times, but how many of our pubs are now restaurants with bars?

HURLEY: *YE OLDE BELL*

Take the Maidenhead-to-Henley road (A423). There is a signpost to Hurley pointing to the right. Meander through the village. Ye Olde Bell is on the right.

There is an almost regal atmosphere to the extremely ancient village of Hurley. There has been some type of settlement here since the Bronze Age. It is described in Domesday Book, and the sister of Edward the Confessor is reputed to be buried here.

Just after the Norman invasion, Hurley's priory was founded or adapted by Geoffrey De Mandeville as a cell of the Benedictine abbey of Westminster. The monastery survived until agents of Henry VIII wreaked havoc during the Reformation. Various parts of the old, dismembered buildings still adorn the village.

Not far from the monastery's massive dovecotes, and acting as a guest house, Ye Olde Bell Inn was erected in 1135. It has provided sustenance ever since then, and is one of half a dozen such buildings claiming to be the oldest inn in the country. Some original parts of the building remain, but much of the Bell is fifteenth century, a mere stripling, just 600 years old.

Until recently Ye Olde Bell was one of four ancient hostelries near the Thames at Hurley. I believe that, sadly, the number is now down to three. As late as the eighteenth century, the inns provided a refuge from the notorious highwaymen and footpads who populated Maidenhead Thicket. It is interesting to note that for decades the vicars of Hurley demanded and received £50 a year as a kind of insurance against being robbed while travelling the Thicket.

The visitor entering Ye Olde Bell today encounters a mass of wooden beams supporting low ceilings, and tortuously twisted passages branching in every conceivable direction. It is difficult to describe the interior any further without

duplicating similar descriptions that apply to a good proportion of the hostelries in this book. One outstanding feature is its massive and ancient fireplace. It is reputed to lead to a tunnel that was used by monks escaping from Henry VIII's agents. Naturally, this has given rise to tales of monks trapped alive and of sounds of ghostly moaning and chanting. Personally, I am sceptical. In the majority of similar instances, the door leads to a wine cellar or a room used for drying logs. We have already met a better-substantiated story of a tunnel at The Chequers in Oxford.

MARLOW: *TWO BREWERS*

The Two Brewers is in St Peter's Street, which runs parallel with Marlow
Bridge, slightly to the east.

The Two Brewers is supposedly named after two brothers who brewed their ale on the premises. The present building, the new one, was erected in 1686. There was obviously another building here before that. St Peter's Road was a main thoroughfare, and at the point where it meets the river was a small wooden bridge on the London-to-Oxford road.

Jane Seymour, one of Henry VIII's wives, is reputed to have lived above Marlow, at Seymour Court. She died with head and body intact, after providing Henry with a son, Edward VI. Unfortunately, Jane died after just a year of marriage. It is not difficult to imagine the future queen crossing the Thames here and journeying to the capital.

In 1835–6 Tierney Clarke constructed a suspension bridge at Marlow. (He also built one between the cities of Buda and Pest in Hungary.) The result of building

Marlow Bridge was to take traffic away from St Peter's Street and onto the High Street. The new bridge had not yet arrived in Shelley's time. He and his wife lived in a red-tiled house in West Street. While he lay on his back and reputedly supped ale at the Two Brewers, his wife Mary was composing her novel, *Frankenstein*.

Another celebrity who almost certainly imbibed at the Two Brewers was John Richardson, the famous entrepreneur showman. Part of Richardson's vast business was a freak show, and one of his exhibits was a 'spotted boy' whom he had brought from the Caribbean (see *A Grim Almanac of Old Berkshire*). The showman developed a special warmth for the boy, and took him to Marlow. The lad died very young and is buried in Marlow churchyard. Later, Richardson joined him there, a strange affinity.

Another regular at the inn was George Payne Rainsford James, a Marlow author and son of a local physician. James sat by the river, engaged in his extremely prolific activity. Apparently, the Two Brewers features, thinly disguised, in several of his works, but in which of his seventy-seven instantly forgettable novels I do not intend to research.

I looked into the Two Brewers on a fine, sunny afternoon. The ancient black beams and low ceilings have survived, but there is now a sort of open games or children's room at the rear. The ambience remains, and the view of the Berkshire side of the Thames is almost magnificent.

Little wonder that Jerome K. Jerome stayed at the Two Brewers while writing that sublime piece of nonsense *Three Men in a Boat*.

COOKHAM: *FERRY HOTEL*

The Ferry Hotel is on the 4094 at Cookham. Stay on the main road. The village lies off to the left.

There is a romantic little story about this old inn, which I first discovered while researching *A Grim Almanac of Old Berkshire*. I repeat it here, unashamedly.

The date was 19 June 1892. The romantic setting of the picturesque Ferry Hotel at Cookham was shattered by the sound of pistol fire. The peace of the gently bobbing boats and the calm reflection of the sun on the rippling Thames was rent asunder by a fat, red-faced man screaming blue murder and yelling for the police.

Only minutes before, serenity had ruled while an attractive, dark-skinned Italian named Pelose played an exquisite, faultless Strauss waltz on the hotel's grand piano. There, beside the watching, waving, weeping willows, Pelose's best friend, the even darker and more handsome Giuseppe Porcolt, danced passionately close to an attractive barmaid.

As the maid gazed into the Italian's eyes, harsh words cut through the air. They were uttered by the hotel's owner, John Billing Kirby, and were to this effect: 'Ain't you ever going to do no bleeding work? There are other customers waiting, you know.'

Porcolt had to do what a gentleman has to do when he has been rudely interrupted. Taking a short pistol from his pocket, he blasted a bullet three inches above the proprietor's head.

Scene two – Reading Assizes: Outcome, guilty of endangering life and misuse of a firearm; six months' hard labour.

Did the pretty barmaid wait for Porcolt, one wonders?

COOKHAM: *BEL AND THE DRAGON*

Cookham is very small. The Bel and Dragon is near the centre of the village.

This is not a misspelling: Bel is the title of Marduk, the ancient patron deity of Babylon. In the story of Bel and the Dragon we are told that Daniel convinced the king that Bel was an image and not a living deity, a type of hologram. Once part of the biblical book of Daniel, the story has been relegated to the Apocrypha, the Septuagint or Esoteric Greek version of events now much contested.

At one time I would have bet money that this was the only inn in Britain with this name. However, while researching this book I noticed a pub as nearby as Windsor with the identical name.

It is said that the Bel and the Dragon was built in 1417. As is the case with many other old inns, it is built on the glebe (church land), and it housed the ever-busy stonemasons. The original wattle and daub walls still exist, but are adequately hidden in most places. The Lady Ferry House once stood nearby but, sadly, is no longer there. Parts of the adjacent packhorse track used by pilgrims, monks and commercial travellers walking from London to Oxford do remain.

I visited the Bel and the Dragon on a June afternoon, and I was pleased to see that the sign of the old apothecary shop was still hanging next door and that the Stanley Spencer gallery still stood opposite. Cookham is justly proud of Spencer, the local artist. In the middle part of the twentieth century he caused much controversy by painting religious scenes in rather an earthy context. The settings were recognisable, some of them featuring landmarks near Cookham.

I enjoyed a pint at one of the rough-hewn wooden tables of the inn. Since my last visit a massive, romantic restaurant has been added at the rear of the building. Once again, it demonstrates the modern preference for dining over wining, but it has been tastefully incorporated and does not look amiss. Possibly less tasteful are the exaggerated, hand-painted cartoons on Australian themes that adorn most of the walls. And the monochrome cartoons in the splendid toilets are a little suspect. In general, the decor is pleasing, albeit a mish-mash – a just acceptable and pleasant mish-mash.

MAIDENHEAD: *BOULTER'S LOCK INN*

The Boulter's Lock Inn lies on the A4094 Maidenhead-to-Cookham road.

Apparently there was a small thirteenth-century bridge on the river here, north of Maidenhead. It has long since disappeared.

When the river became the main route for transporting goods, it was a very chancy business. Many a craft was torn to splinters, and many a boatman drowned in the rapid currents and treacherous weirs. Locks were the answer, and Boulter's

Lock was the first to appear, in 1746. 'Boulter' is a milling term and refers to the activity of boulting or sieving. It is therefore fitting that the lock is built next to an island on which stood Ray Mill. The mill survives and, although much altered, houses the Boulter's Lock Inn or Hotel. I called at the inn on a late June afternoon; little had altered. People were dining on the terrace and watching the boats make their way over the water. This stretch of river was always the most popular. In Victorian times one could walk from the popular Skindles Hotel to Cookham via Boulter's Lock, going from craft to craft without getting one's feet wet. Edward Gregory's famous picture showing a summer day at Boulter's Lock illustrates the chaos and confusion. Occasionally, tempers frayed. In August 1883 a man was charged with assaulting the lock-keeper after having to wait two and a half hours to enter the lock (see *A Grim Almanac of Old Berkshire*).

On the afternoon of my visit all was peace and quiet, except for the throb of diesel engines. I crossed the small bridge, with its memorial stone stating that Richard Dimbleby, probably our most distinguished commentator (the father of David and Jonathan), had lived at nearby Mill Head Island House for decades. On entering the old flour mill (converted in 1950), I noted that the ancient sign-cum-advertisement for Ascot Sunday at Boulter's Lock was slightly faded. I lifted my glass to the figures in Gregory's riverscape above the bar, and retired to the terrace.

MAIDENHEAD: *THAMES HOTEL*

The Thames Hotel is situated on the A4095, the lower Cookham Road, which runs parallel to the Thames.

This upmarket hotel on the banks of the Thames has a tenuous association with a famous murder. It was not committed here, but this was a favourite watering hole of the victim.

Towards the end of the nineteenth century, Mrs Minnie Freeman-Lee was a beautiful celebrity, toasted by the high society of Europe. In 1908 she was married to a solicitor and living in a seventeen-room house in Maidenhead. Minnie was deprived of her son in the First World War, and her husband died in the 1930s. The property, now inhabited by a lone Minnie, fell into disrepair, and in 1948, at the age of 88, she was living in one room. However, a rumour persisted that she was sitting on a gold mine. This was far from the truth. Minnie's one luxury in life was to have lunch once or twice a week at the Thames Hotel. On 1 June 1948 milkman George Rome, seeing yesterday's milk still on the doorstep, decided to investigate. Accompanied by a neighbour, Arthur Hilsdon, he searched every trophy-filled room in the house but could find no sign of Minnie. They decided that it was a matter for the police.

Later, when Minnie's solicitor and neighbours carried out a more thorough search in the company of the local police, the young solicitor played with the fastenings on

a trunk. Suddenly the lid flew open, exposing the bound and gagged dead body of Minnie Freeman-Lee.

'The Maidenhead Trunk Murder' was taken up by the media. At the post-mortem the cause of death was found to be asphyxiation. The famous Superintendent Chapman of the Flying Squad took over the case. Later he called upon the assistance of Chief Superintendent Cherrill ('Cherub'), the country's greatest expert on fingerprints. After many hours of concentrated effort Cherrill could find nothing: the murderer had used gloves. Finally, under the bed, on the top of a small jewellery box, he found the prints of two fingertips, each just ⁵⁄₁₆in long.

The prints were matched to those of George Russell, an Irish labourer who had been known to the police since 1933. Within a week Russell was in custody, having been arrested at a hostel in St Albans. In his possession was a scarf belonging to Minnie Freeman-Lee. It was soon discovered that he had been working as a jobbing gardener at Maidenhead at the time of Minnie's death. At Reading Assizes, before Mr Justice Hallet, Russell virtually convicted himself with words to the effect, 'Why would I murder an old woman in a house that contained nothing of value?'

The jury was out for two hours, longer than expected, but returned with a guilty verdict. George Russell was hanged at Oxford on 2 December 1948.

The Thames Hotel opened in the late 1880s. In the early days it had a colourful existence. Wining, dining and rather reckless gambling were the norm. The building

Chief Superintendent Cherrill.

was one of the earliest telegraph offices, and aristocratic players were thus able to wire home for more money. A booklet produced by the hotel's owners informs us that one proprietor lost his property's freehold on the turn of one card.

Nowadays guests are a little less reckless with their money, but the building is just as plush. On a summer's evening cocktails in the River Bar and dinner in the Moorings, followed by a good bottle of wine on the terrace, are experiences not to be missed.

MAIDENHEAD: *BEAR HOTEL*

The Bear stands near the eastern end of Maidenhead High Street.

There is a definite shortage of olde worlde inns in Maidenhead. The Bear Hotel is one of the few exceptions. It stands near the end of the High Street, and the massive figure of a black bear is almost ostentatious.

The Bear has a chequered history. Tom Middleton, in the popular book *Royal Berkshire*, states that in 1489 the landlord was charged with demanding unlawful prices. He was no doubt taking advantage of a captive clientele. Maidenhead Thicket had a terrible reputation for violence and robbery, even before the era when the stagecoaches traversed it. Better to pay a high price for a hotel than to pay with one's life at the Thicket.

What is probably the best-known tale of The Bear occurred at the old inn's original site, 35 High Street. The king (we do not know which one) became separated from his hunting party and roamed alone into the hamlet of Maidenhead. Unrecognised, he entered the inn and ordered dinner. The landlord apologised and

pointed out that he could not serve his customer. As it was Lent, no meat was permitted, and his small supply of fish had been ordered by the two gentlemen in the corner, the vicar of Bray and his curate. The king suggested that the landlord ask the reverend gentlemen if he could dine with them. The vicar grudgingly consented. However, he soon found his guest to be witty and congenial. The trouble came when the bill arrived and the king pointed out he had no money about his person. The vicar was greatly affronted, but the curate stated that he would gladly pay the stranger's share of the bill in return for the good company he had provided. At that moment the king's hunting party arrived in search of him. Immediately recognising his dinner companion, the vicar fell to his knees and begged forgiveness. The king, a compassionate man, forgave the cleric and assured him that he would keep his position at Bray. The curate was given a vacant canonry at Windsor.

A less whimsical story of The Bear tells of a fire at the inn. It happened in 1835, towards the end of the coaching era. No fewer than thirty-five horses were burned to death in the tragic blaze, only one horse surviving. Aptly named Miraculous, he went on to work for many years, pulling the Bristol Mail.

Today The Bear is a browsers' paradise; I can think of few better places to enjoy a Scotch and a cigar while viewing the multitude of paintings on its walls.

One final anecdote. The hotel foyer was once home to a large stuffed bear, which was kidnapped by some day-trippers from the Isle of Wight. It resurfaced on the island at a museum, where the curator had bought him in good faith. At one stage delicate negotiations for its return were afoot, but I do not know their outcome.

BRAY: *HINDS HEAD HOTEL*

To find the Hinds Head Hotel is simplicity itself. It is situated at the top of Bray's brief High Street.

I stopped here on a warm June day and sat, with my beer, on a seat near the door with a fine view down Bray's unchanging High Street.

The origin of this ancient building and the function for which it was built are matters of speculation. One school of thought is that it was a hunting lodge, another is that it was built to house stonemasons working on St Michael's church. Personally, I go for a compromise. It was probably built for one purpose and adapted for another.

As a teenager, in the 1960s, I was a regular at the inn, hoping to rub shoulders with the film stars who frequented it. When I returned in the 1990s, little had changed, and it appears that little has changed now. There are still the low beams and the cross-members supported by rough-hewn props, and the odd sedan chair is still in evidence. I did not notice the newspaper clippings stating that the Queen and Prince Philip had dropped in, or another announcing that Bray village would close for the burial of George III. However, the bar was crowded, and I may have missed them.

The vast old fireplace is still a conversation piece, and the placard giving a potted history of the infamous vicar of Bray is still in situ. Again, there is a difference of opinion as to who the famous vicar was. In the immortal song that has come down the centuries the first line, 'In good King Charles's golden days', implies that the vicar was Francis Carswell, who is buried in the churchyard. It is claimed that he changed his religious allegiance four times so as to remain the vicar of Bray. His words, quoted in the chorus, state,

> And this is law, I will maintain
> Until my dying day, Sir.
> That whatsoever King may reign,
> I will be the vicar of Bray, Sir!

However, the consensus seems to favour an ecclesiastical gentleman named Simon Aleyn, who was twice a Catholic and twice a Protestant during the reigns of Henry VIII and his three children. Aleyn had witnessed martyrs being burned to death at Windsor. This probably encouraged his flexible attitude towards religion.

I shall end with some words of wisdom engraved across the fireplace of the Hinds Head: 'Fear knocked the door. Faith answered and there was nobody there.' What do you think of that sentiment, Mr Aleyn, Mr Carswell? Not a lot.

BRAY: *MONKEY ISLAND HOTEL*

The Monkey Island Hotel is in Monkey Island Lane, but it is difficult to find. Even the brochure only gives the address as Bray and nothing else. There is a small insignificant signpost in the centre of the village, but it is easier to ask a local.

Monkey Island, probably originally Monks Eyot, is a 4-acre site close to the charming and expensive village of Bray. The island lies in the centre of the Thames and can be reached only by a footbridge. It is well worth a visit, but more than a little crowded in the summer.

There are two buildings on the island, one of them being the plush Monkey Island Hotel. The building was originally a fishing lodge, erected by Charles Spencer in the early 1700s. In 1733 this dissolute playboy inherited the Dukedom of Marlborough from his ageing aunt Henrietta, and decided to reform the monotony of tradition and renovate the fishing lodge. The rococo style of early eighteenth-century French architecture afforded a certain amount of fun and freedom to the designers. Internally artists experimented with paintings of animals in human situations. Monkeys, being man's nearest cousins, were frequently depicted in hunting, shooting and fishing scenes. The ceiling of the hotel was painted by De Clermont. Monkeys, well dressed in eighteenth-century attire, are engaged in a variety of human activities. It has been suggested, but with little verification, that Monkey Island was the inspiration for Pierre Boulle's *Planet of the Apes*.

In 1905 royalty were entertained at Monkey Island, when King Edward VII and Queen Adelaide cruised down the river from their boathouse at Datchet for after-noon tea.

On my most recent visit to Monkey Island, I enquired where the peacocks had gone. 'They used to fight with the swans and geese, and they also woke up the guests,' I was told.

I was given a postcard of the Monkey Room, and informed that there is a hidden face in the picture.

OAKLEY GREEN: *OAKLEY COURT HOTEL*

The Oakley Court Hotel stands on the Windsor-to-Maidenhead road (A308) at Oakley Green.

This is yet another building that is far too prestigious to be termed an inn. The Gothic mansion stands beside the river in the tiny village of Oakley Green, roughly midway between Maidenhead and Windsor. On a summer's day the great lawns that sweep down to the Thames proclaim a noble ambience. It was not always so.

Sir Robert Saye built Oakley Court as a private mansion in 1858. Saye was certainly an eccentric, so far as architecture is concerned. Bizarre is probably the best description for the building. The twisted towers are ominous and overpowering; the weird gargoyles that look down have been described as the intimidating creations of an anomalous mind. Seen on a misty day or a stormy night it might appear as an archetypal recreation of Gothic, spine-chilling terror. Strong words? Maybe so, but the architecture lent itself so well to the horror-movie image that the Hammer film company used it as a setting for movies of the Dracula and Frankenstein type for almost twenty years. The outlandish exterior, cloaked in manufactured mist, became the hallmark of the company.

During the Second World War the Government took over Oakley Court and loaned it to the French Resistance. The old building was wrapped in a veil of secrecy. However, it was difficult to find local labour; people avoided the house like the plague. Those courageous enough to remain complained of all sorts of strange phenomena, and the electrics had a life of their own.

From the mid-1950s to the mid-1970s the building was derelict. I remember it well. If the structure had looked bizarre when inhabited, it looked grotesquely moribund when left to decay for twenty years. Local teenagers dared each other to spend the night there, and during this period a local journalist insisted that local people found the atmosphere so oppressive that they had committed suicide in the Thames. The report is probably extremely exaggerated. But, strangely enough, several people did commit suicide within sight of Oakley Court during that time, although it was probably a coincidence.

Oakley Court became a hotel in 1982. Extra buildings were added, and it has become one of the most sumptuous, grand, luxurious, lavish experiences one can enjoy.

WINDSOR: *YE HARTE & GARTER* (*once Star and Garter*)

Ye Harte & Garter is situated near the junction of the High Street and Thames Street. It is close to the station, Peascod Street and opposite Windsor Castle.

To liken Ye Harte & Garter to a pub would be akin to describing Buckingham Palace as a fine detached house. To have taken a room here for the night of the wedding of the Prince of Wales and Camilla Parker Bowles would have cost me four months' salary.

Let us take a brief look at some other events the hotel has witnessed. Late in the year 1579 the Windsor Witches were arrested near the Star and Garter. Several of them lived in hovels close to the main streets. Elizabeth Styles (alias Rockingham), Mother Duttel, Mother Devell and Mother Margaret were arraigned, condemned and executed at Abingdon.

In 1629 a very sad story emerged from the old inn. James Dean, a boy just 8 years old, was found guilty of setting fire to two of the Star and Garter's outhouses.

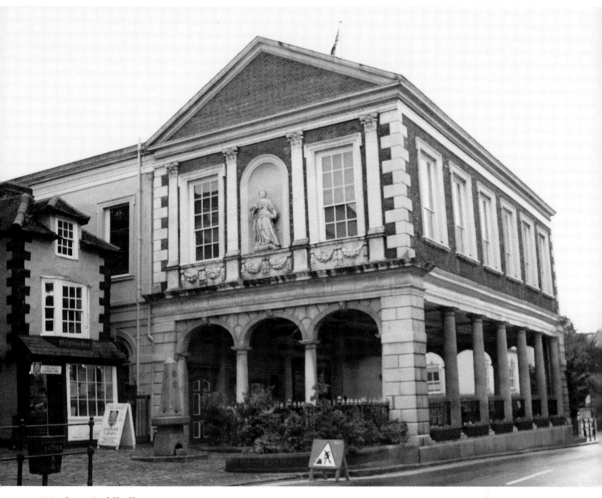

Windsor Guildhall.

Queen Victoria stayed in Windsor. *(Illustrated London News)*

He was hanged for the crime and is thought to be the youngest person ever to have been executed in England.

In 1831 a lighter sentence was passed on two under-wrappers, Smith and Papps, who were fined 2s for cutting part-way through a harness. Apparently they had been none too pleased with their tips.

In 1882 Roderick McClean shot at Queen Victoria in Windsor, and missed. He was wrestled to the ground and was held briefly at the Star and Garter. After being found not guilty by reason of insanity, he spent the rest of his days in Broadmoor.

Another occasion on which the Star and Garter was filled to capacity was in 1939, when George Henry Willis was charged with the murder of 85-year-old Henry Paul in his one-roomed shanty at Winkfield. Paul sold his own produce on Windsor Bridge, and, as he had been a very popular man, the media had a field day. The preliminary hearing was held at Windsor Guildhall, which was in no way large enough, so it was moved to Reading. More details of this sensational trial are described in *A Grim Almanac of Old Berkshire*.

WINDSOR: *SIR CHRISTOPHER WREN'S HOUSE HOTEL*

Sir Christopher Wren's House Hotel is directly opposite Windsor Bridge on the south side overlooking the river.

As its name suggests, this immaculate old building was erected and inhabited by England's greatest architect, the creator of St Paul's Cathedral. This is probably the most romantic hotel on the River Thames. The place has an undeniable

ambience. Strok's restaurant, overlooking the river, is perfect for the young beau bent on impressing his date. The cocktail bar and adjoining lounge have an air of unashamed opulence. The benign feeling of style and comfort belies the rather sombre history of the hotel, which for many years was thought to be cursed.

The hotel was once a private house belonging to the Cheshire family. Unfortunate family members would be struck down suddenly by mysterious and fatal illnesses. They were afflicted by deadly tropical diseases, endemic to foreign countries to which they had never travelled.

The sad events of the family were not restricted to illness and disease. One of the daughters had a severe mental breakdown after giving birth to an illegitimate child. The child died in infancy, and the mother never recovered. She was held under house arrest and permitted the freedom of the garden only in the very early or late hours of the day. Mr Cheshire nearly died of food poisoning – whether accidental or otherwise is unknown. The unfortunate man then found that his fortune was rapidly decreasing, and so he moved into a smaller property. This may have had a bearing on the case of another of his daughters. The lass, who was engaged to a peer, was jilted overnight.

The curse appears to have been attached to the property rather than to the family. A stream of tenants came and went over the next hundred years. One of these was Baroness Vaux, who used the building as a summer residence in the early 1900s. The Baroness could retain no staff; all left after a few days, complaining that the atmosphere in parts of the building was unbearable. It is not known when the Baroness left, but the building remained empty for a number of years following the termination of her occupancy.

In the 1930s Wren's house was purchased by two sisters with the unusual name of Outlaw. They turned it into a teashop and later into a hotel. There has been nothing but the most pleasant of atmosphere in the place ever since.

ETON: *WATERMAN'S ARMS*

The Waterman's Arms is in Brocas Street. Cross Windsor Bridge from the Windsor side to Eton. Turn left as soon as possible.

The Waterman's Arms is still a pub, a rarity in Windsor and Eton, which are arguably the two prettiest towns on the river. On either side of the Thames, any available hostelry has been bought up by the conglomerates, extended, depersonalised, stripped of character, or turned into a Thai restaurant. The Waterman's Arms has acquired a vast restaurant since I last visited many years ago. However, it has been tastefully done and is in keeping with the rest of the building.

The place was very busy when I called in towards the end of June 2005. I was pleased to see that most of the old paintings, prints and photographs on the walls have survived. They depict local scenes; Windsor Castle, Eton College and Clifton Chapel are obviously to the fore. There used to be prints of boating scenes, and I trust they are still there, but one is a little reluctant to disturb the patrons by gazing at the walls close to their seats.

What seemed to be new – new to me anyway – was a map or chart of the river, painted in bright blue, on the ceiling. Postcards have been placed on the map in the appropriate geographical locations. I leaned on the bar, quaffing a pint and wondering why there was a map of Falmouth Harbour on the wall.

Just in case this description sounds a little too serene, let me add just a couple of lines about the inn's history. The Waterman's Arms was built in about 1542 and was soon adopted as a plague house. The dead and dying were floated down the Thames on rafts, to be interred in its foundations. There have been no reports of ghostly moanings for decades. So one can sit down to relax in The Waterman's, and enjoy a substantial meal and a full-bodied beer.

DATCHET: *ROYAL STAG*

The Royal Stag is not difficult to find. It is at the eastern end of Datchet's short High Street.

It is time for a ghost story. Datchet is as old as history. It was ancient when Shakespeare knew it. He gave Falstaff his ducking in Datchet Mead. The church is fourteenth century, and the inn next door is not much younger. The Royal Stag has been renovated many times, but much of the ancient outer structure survives. The story goes that a labourer stopped by for a drink on his way home from work. It was a freezing cold night and the attractive village was covered in snow. The workman left his young son outside while he slaked his thirst and passed a convivial evening with his friends. Before long the workman's brain was befuddled and he had lost all trace of time and memory of his young lad.

After playing some youthful games, the lad had become wet and cold. He knocked in vain on the window on the inn, but did not succeed in attracting the attention of his hapless father. Having failed in this, he tried to enter the adjacent church, but either it was locked or the door was too heavy for him to move it. The poor lad's lifeless body was found in a snowdrift against the church wall.

The ghostly hand print that periodically appears at the inn's window is said to be the spectre of the child's futile plea for help.

Photographs of the reputed handprint have been taken over the years, and in 1979 the glass was removed for examination by a national newspaper. Mysteriously, the print disappeared from the original pane, only to manifest itself on the one that replaced it.

I have read that in 1966 the gravestone of one William Herbert was discovered in the cellar. As there have been several tolerably famous William Herberts in history, I am not certain which of them is represented by the stone. It may, of course, be some, mute inglorious Milton, some local son of the soil. Suffice to say that, if the gravestone is removed, all sorts of terrible prophecies will be acted out. I have been unable to discover whether it is still there.

OLD WINDSOR: *BELLS OF OUSLEY*

Straight Road is part of the A308 from Staines to Windsor. The Bells is on the corner of Straight Road and Ousley Road.

This lovely old Thameside pub has recently been taken over by a restaurant chain. It is now smart, clean, efficient, spotless and characterless.

Once the tale of the Bells of Ousley was proclaimed on its walls, but, so far as I can tell, it is no longer. The story is brief: there was once a monastery at Ousley, near Old Windsor. Hearing of Henry VIII's Reformation and his destruction of the monasteries, the brothers, realising that the building was doomed, strived to save the bells.

A raft was constructed and the bells were removed from the tower and dragged to the banks of the Thames. The intention was to float them across to a small island just off Old Windsor. The monks set out under cover of darkness, but it was not long before the raft capsized, spilling the heavy bells into the river. History records that they were never retrieved, but the Thames is neither broad nor deep here. One wonders, what did happen to the famous Bells of Ousley?

STAINES: *SWAN HOTEL*

*The Swan Hotel is in The Hythe, a tiny road that overlooks the waterfront,
adjacent to Staines Bridge.*

Staines has been totally modernised. It is not unattractive, and the riverside walks
with their stainless-steel figures are quite fetching. Modern pubs, such as the
Outback and Ha Ha's, beneath massive blocks of flats, are fine and dandy for serving
the masses, but there is obviously no history there.

The Thames Hotel is ancient, but has been completely altered. Modern art
surrounds the lounge. Some old cartoons on the theme of camping along the
Thames hang in the toilets, but there is nothing from which a story could be made.
South of the river, the Jolly Farmer is ancient but small, with nothing recorded, and
the Anne Boleyn shares the same fate.

The beautiful old Swan Hotel must have a history, but the manager knew nothing
and there was nothing mentioned on his computer. Why is it that the proprietors of
these old inns, which must be steeped in history, never research it and inform their
customers?

The little knowledge I have been able to glean is as follows. The Swan stands by
Staines Bridge, which was constructed by John Rennie, the Scottish civil engineer,

who was also responsible for Southwark Bridge, London Bridge and the original Waterloo Bridge. Rennie stayed at The Swan and, apart from designing bridges, he worked on plans for canals in the area. The Kennet and Avon canal was said to have been planned here. Not far from Rennie's bridge is a stone marking the former limit of the Corporation of London Authority's jurisdiction over the Thames.

Little has changed at The Swan since Rennie's day. The atmosphere is enchanting, from the horse and dog collars outside, through the softly lit bar, past the open fireplace to the superb riverside restaurant. It is a romantic hotel. Perhaps Samuel Pepys found it so. He wrote some of his famous diary here, while looking over the peaceful Thames.

CHERTSEY: *THE GEORGE*

The George is in the centre of Chertsey in Guildford Street. It is best to find a central car park and walk.

The George began life in the fourteenth century, as a hunting lodge, and became an inn about one hundred years later. Although there have been changes, the building has weathered and resisted the supposed financial rewards of modernisation. There are rumours of an underground passage here, and one, if not two, priest's holes exist. Naturally, Dick Turpin called here, and there is also a rumour of a bulky female ghost who makes dents in beds.

A third unsubstantiated rumour is that a relative of Rose Hartwick Thorpe stayed here and took back to the United States an outdated sugary book called *Love and Loyalty*. This caused the poet from Indiana to compose a remarkably bad poem that she based in Chertsey. It has now become a legend of the town.

The poem 'Curfew must not Ring Tonight' is based on an incident during the Wars of the Roses in which the Duke of Warwick's nephew was captured by Yorkists and imprisoned at Chertsey. Knowing that her lover was to die at curfew that evening, the heroine, Plucky Blanche, clung onto the bell's clapper so that the bell could not be heard by the townspeople and the conveniently deaf sexton. Bloodied and battered, but deliriously happy, Blanche placed a reprieve at the feet of the sergeant-at-arms. As in all good fairy stories, everybody lived happily ever after.

When the story crossed the Atlantic, the Wars of the Roses became Cromwell's Civil War, Blanche became Bessie and Warwick's young nephew became Basil. It was so bad that it had to be a hit in the USA. Here are a few lines:

> Still the maiden, clinging firmly
> Quivering lip and fair face white,
> Stilled her frightened heart's wild throbbing:
> 'Curfew shall not ring tonight!'

Later, comedians took over and changed the poem into a crude song, by which time Bessie had metamorphosed into Nellie.

> Hang on the bell, Nellie, hang on the bell
> Your lover is locked in a cold prison cell
> As she swings to the left and swings to the right
> Remember, curfew must not ring tonight.

At least the song, unlike the poem, had the good grace not to take itself seriously. Think. If Blanche/Bessie/Nellie had had the sense to tie a load of sacking around the clapper, she would have saved herself a lot of discomfort. I admit the storyline would have suffered a little.

WEYBRIDGE: *THE GROTTO*

The Grotto is on Monument Hill, which bears to the right at the eastern end of the High Street.

Weybridge is another historic town on the Thames. Obviously, it takes its name from a bridge on the River Wey. There has been a bridge here since 1235. There is also a tradition at Weybridge that Caesar crossed the Thames here in 55 BC. The town once possessed a splendid palace, Oatlands. But this beautiful building stands no more. Henry VIII built it for his fourth wife, Anne of Cleves. Unfortunately, Anne did not live long, but at least Oatlands was much admired and appreciated by Catherine Howard, Henry's fifth wife. Oatlands was demolished during the Civil War. Later, stones from the ruins of the palace were used in the construction of the Wey Navigational Canal.

The grounds, laid out by the Duke of Newcastle in the mid-1700s, lasted somewhat longer than the palace. The Duke created a mile-long lake and spent £40,000 on a unique grotto. He imported a father-and-son team from Italy. They spent thirty years at Weybridge, decorating the walls with minerals, crystals and horses' teeth.

The Grotto public house, named after the Duke's construction, is thought to have been the laundry of the former Oatlands Palace. Many years ago a vast inglenook held an open fireplace here. Rumour has it that one evening a customer was leaning on the wall near the inglenook. 'This wall is exceedingly warm,' he declared. It was discovered that the main beam, essential to holding up the house, had been smouldering for years. The inglenook was bricked up for safety reasons. Legend insists that the builders engaged on the work found an underground passage to Oatlands Palace.

WEYBRIDGE: *SHIP HOTEL*

The Ship Hotel is situated at the eastern end of Weybridge High Street, opposite the monument.

The ancient town of Weybridge has lost many of its old hostelries over the last couple of decades. Fortunately, The Ship remains. It has been much altered over the years and has completely swallowed up several adjacent buildings. One gave it a touch of indigestion, as we shall read later.

There are several stories associated with The Ship, but I had to go to many sources to uncover them. In the eighteenth century the Duchess of York used this old inn when she visited her beloved Weybridge. Another celebrated lady who was no stranger to The Ship was Fanny Kemble, the nineteenth-century actress, authoress and playwright. Here, Robert Louis Stevenson pondered over the proofs of *Treasure Island*, arguably the schoolboy's greatest adventure.

A tall column stands on the green opposite the inn, placed there as a tribute to the Duchess of York. The pillar once stood at Seven Dials in London. It was pulled down by rioters, who mistakenly thought that treasure was buried beneath it. The

fallen column was purchased by a Weybridge builder and remained in his yard for some time. After the death of the popular Duchess, the landlord of the Ship Hotel, Joseph Todd, raised a subscription to have it erected on the green. Todd was an astute businessman: people flocked to see the new landmark. Todd ran coaches to Weybridge, transport for thirsty people who paid for sustenance at his inn.

Among the many customers who visited The Ship was one uninvited one, who was far less popular than the rest. In the early days a chapel adjoined the inn. An ostler hanged himself from one of its beams. The unfortunate man's ghost was said to haunt the building. As suicide was discouraged, it was not long before the local clergy deconsecrated the building and closed it. The Ship's landlord (possibly Todd) was always on the look-out for bargains. He bought the old chapel and incorporated it into the inn. Under the communal roof there was a gap, and Frances D. Stewart, a popular writer of ghost stories, suggests that this gave the spectral ostler a chance to slip into The Ship. Once upon a time he was witnessed regularly, but nothing has been seen of him lately.

SHEPPERTON: *THE ANCHOR*

The Anchor is in Church Square, off Church Road, which is the A375 to Chertsey.

This is a large and attractive hotel in the benign old town of Shepperton. An exact translation of Shepperton is sheep town, but it seems to have attracted more film stars than sheep of late.

The film stars' favourite, The Anchor, lies in the romantic Church Square. When I arrived one Saturday lunchtime there were several weddings in progress. One set of guests had ensconced itself in The Anchor and another was firmly in situ at the King's Head opposite. This was England at its best, people in their finery, enjoying the warm weather, in an antiquated town square outside two ancient inns, with the sound of bells pealing out from an even more ancient church. I would not have been surprised to have seen Steed, Emma Peel or Simon Templar among the guests.

The Anchor is a hotel for romance. It certainly was for Elizabeth Taylor and Richard Burton; they courted here while making a film at Shepperton Studios. In earlier days Lord Nelson and Lady Hamilton were known to patronise The Anchor – as did Charles Dickens, who seems to have been the only celebrity who did not conduct a clandestine affair here. On the grim side, the old inn was supposedly a haunt of Dick Turpin. Excuse my scepticism, but, after exploring over 5,000 old inns, I find it far easier to name those at which the famous footpad did not stay. His shade haunts about 150 pubs that I know of. Perhaps there is some substance in the old adage 'No peace for the wicked'.

Dick was a cowardly blackguard of the worst order. He was also very forgetful. I have been shown three of his hats, two neckerchiefs, two horsewhips and here, at

The Anchor, they have his pistol – found in the rafters. The weapon is thought to be Turpin's because it has 'Dick's friend' inscribed upon it. Could it possibly have belonged to one of the estimated 125,000 Dicks who populated the south of England at the time?

SHEPPERTON: *KING'S HEAD*

The King's Head stands directly opposite The Anchor in Church Square.

The King's Head is fifteenth century and looks it. This enchanting old building was patronised by Charles I and Nell Gwynne when they visited Windsor. As with The Anchor, this also was a little hideaway for Richard Burton and Elizabeth Taylor.

One feels really relaxed at the King's Head. Although the frontage is quite contained, the bars, one behind the other, go back a surprisingly long way. The back bar contains a bistro-type area that overlooks an attractive garden.

During the coaching era the King's Head became a stagecoach station. Apparently a large number of horses would stand in Church Square, awaiting their turns to pull the very regular coaches. Little seems to have changed over the centuries; the low, oak-beamed ceilings remain, as do the stone and rough timber floors. The vast inglenook fireplace is frequently a conversation piece; long may it remain so.

There was a popular wedding in progress when I visited the King's Head. This made it difficult to take in much of the decor, but I did notice one thing worth mentioning, a more recent conversation piece than the ancient inglenook. It is an England football shirt in a glass case. So far as I can make out, it has been signed by the whole squad. After a very brief chat with the very busy landlord/barman I understood that it was from the 2001/2 season.

HAMPTON: *BELL INN*

The Bell at Hampton stands on the Upper Sunbury Road, at Thames Street, opposite the river.

After the exquisite olde worlde exterior, with its high windows overlooking the Thames, the interior of the Bell Inn is something of culture shock. It is spacious (I imagine several rooms have been knocked into one), but it has been so modernised as to make a complete contrast to the exterior. It has been nicely and efficiently done, but it is not for me. Most of the ground floor is a tapas bar – incidentally, the young couple next to me had dispensed with the menu and were eating each other. I wonder what old Fred Karno would make of it. Fred stayed here regularly.

I will expound a little on Fred Karno and his army at Tagg's Island. Tagg's Island is just a stone's throw from The Bell. Frederick Wescott, better known as Fred Karno, was born in Exeter in 1866. After beginning work as a plumber, Fred started his showbiz career as an acrobat and gymnast. He, with two others, formed the Three Karnos, which later became Fred Karno's Army. Fred became a very wealthy man

and socialised with people such as Charlie Chaplin and Harry Weldon. Capitalising on such friends, Fred became a household name on both sides of the Atlantic.

In 1912 Fred's financial status enabled him to purchase Tagg's Island, a scruffy, run-down place in the Thames near Hampton. Tagg's Island had been the home of local gypsies for generations. Fred evicted them, incurring many curses in the process. The gypsies were in the way of Fred's ambitious plans for the island. His ideas for his millionaire's playground included a hotel, a luxurious restaurant, theatre, ballroom and some splendid gardens. Unfortunately Fred went bankrupt in 1926, probably more through adventurous investments than as a result of gypsy curses. He owed £16,000 – a phenomenal sum in those days. Not only that, he had also lost his comic genius and was ageing rapidly. His wife died in 1927, and he married Marie Moore, who had been his mistress for over a quarter of a century. The musical king died in obscurity in 1941 at his off-licence in Dorset. He left just £42.

Fred's island paradise, Karisono (Tagg's Island), was still the 'in place' in the late 1920s and early 1930s. Among the rich and famous guests was Brooklands racing hero Tommy Hann. In 1923 and 1924 Hann swept everything before him in the motor racing field, but by the 1930s he was a has-been. Working as an experimental engineer, Tommy invested all his money in a car that he practically built himself. It turned out to be a dismal failure. Soon afterwards Tommy was found gassed in his flat in Holland Park Avenue. Shortly before his suicide he had confided to his friends that he had lost his nerve after his best friend's wife had lost her life when the car they were in slipped off the Tagg's Island Ferry. Despite having dived many times into the water, he had failed to rescue the lady. It had affected him very badly.

HAMPTON COURT: *KING'S ARMS*

The King's Arms stands opposite the entrance to Bushy Park in Hampton Court Road.

This stalwart three-storeyed building stands opposite the entrance to Bushy Park. It is literally an inn for all seasons. Ancient as the hills, it has a couple of attractive bars that are well in keeping with the antiquated hostelry.

It is time for a personal story, and a ghostly one at that.

While I was researching *Haunted Inns of Surrey* I was directed to the King's Arms. I mentioned my mission to Tim, the landlord.

'Ghosts?' he said, 'How many do you want?'

'How many have you got?' I asked.

'About half a dozen,' came the reply.

Tim gave me a tour of the house, explaining where each spook lived. There was certainly a very strange atmosphere in one of the cellars; the barmaids would not go down there. Another cellar was unused and therefore had no light. We crept about, the torch faltering, as I was shown a chair that shifted itself from whatever position it was placed in. I think my companion/photographer got the biggest shock when I emerged, ghostly white – literally covered in cobwebs!

Tim finished the tour by showing me the second-storey room where a young lad, after finding that his mother had committed suicide, had ended his own life by jumping from the window. The lad, or possibly the mother, is thought to haunt that room.

Some time afterwards a local radio station invited me to do a programme from the King's Arms and half a dozen other spooky pubs. We were working live from the inn, but alterations were in progress so we could not go up to the haunted second-floor bedroom, or any room on the first floor; all were occupied.

Never at a loss for improvisation, my interviewer decided that we should stand at the ground-floor casement and pretend we were in the ghost room on the second floor. All went well until the interviewer said to me, 'Think of the poor lad hurling himself to the ground'.

I got the giggles and said, 'It wouldn't do him a lot of harm, we're only two feet from the ground!'

The sound was cut.

EAST MOLESEY: *THE BELL*

The Bell is in St Mary's Road, off Spencer Road, which is south of Walton.

Off the beaten track, but close to Hampton Court, stands The Bell. To be exact, it seems to lean rather than stand. The Bell is known as 'The Crooked House'. Centuries of its weight pulling on the timbers have twisted them until every window and gable seem threateningly askew. The overall effect defies written description and must be seen to be believed.

The Bell is some 550 years old and looks every day of it. Claude Duval, the French gentleman highwayman, is purported to have hidden here from the authorities after a hold-up. Hence the Duval bar and the Runner's bar. This makes a change from Dick Turpin, who has been reported to patronise before his death, and to haunt after his demise, literally hundreds of pubs in parts of the country he never even visited.

The Bell seems justifiably proud of its past. In one of its many twisted small rooms (there does not seem to be a right angle in the whole building) there is a notice stating that the building once also served as a post office. Another note refers to the effigy of a naval officer that decorates the weather vane on top of the building. Apparently the officer is on very extended loan from the neighbouring church, the spyglass in his hand being used to search for his missing congregation. Look no further, sir – they are all in The Bell.

THAMES DITTON: *YE OLDE SWAN*

Ye Olde Swan is in Riversdale, off Summer Road, which is a continuation of Thames Ditton High Street.

Thames Ditton, like its nearby sister Long Ditton, derives its name from the Anglo-Saxon 'dictun', meaning a farm by a dyke.

The village is not short of ancient hostelries. At least five remain, and a few decades ago there were several more. The oldest of them is Ye Olde Swan. It stands

by the river, as it has done for 600 years. My only complaint is that parking is a nightmare. This was not a problem when I first visited the inn in the 1960s. In those days one just pulled up at the door and ordered a pint, having first been greeted by the tinny voice of a cockatoo called Charlie.

Countless celebrities must have patronised The Swan over the centuries, but the record is lost in the mists of time. One name that has survived, however, is that of Thomas Hood, the early nineteenth-century poet. Known as the Pauper's Poet, Hood fell in love with The Swan and stayed here on a regular basis. He became successful after writing 'The Dream of Eugene Aram', a poem about a real-life murder. Even better known is his 'The Song of the Shirt', which he wrote while staying at The Swan. It is a tale of poverty, make do and mend. Here are some of its most poignant lines:

> With fingers weary and worn,
> With eyelids heavy and red,
> A woman sits in unwomanly rags,
> Plying her needle and thread.
> Stitch! stitch! stitch!
> In poverty, hunger, and dirt,
> And still with a voice of dolorous pitch
> She sang the 'Song of the Shirt'.

I called at The Swan in June 2005; it was too packed to enjoy the aesthetic charm of place. However, I was also there in the winter of 2004. Nothing seemed to have changed much; the massive fireplace was still there. We took bets that an Australian barmaid could not get a fire going in five minutes. She did it in three. I was most impressed.

THAMES DITTON: *GEORGE AND DRAGON*

The George and Dragon is centrally situated in the High Street.

This is an attractive pub on a bend of the river. Do not be put off by what appears to be limited parking; there is a large car park at the back. I called here on a pleasant day in June 2005, and people were dining at the generous-sized tables outside. Inside, there are a couple of spacious bars, and local scenes are displayed on the walls – including some photos of the Thames in flood.

In 1867 the first bicycles began to appear, but cycling really took off later in the century, after the invention of the pneumatic tyre. Women were as adventurous as men. How they mounted their machines, adorned in corsets, mutton-sleeved blouses, stiff collars and ties and button-up boots is a mystery. Add to this their flowing skirts, in constant danger of tangling in the chains, and you had a recipe for disaster.

When cycling clubs were the vogue the three main societies in Surrey were at Guildford, Ripley and Thames Ditton. Thames Ditton was the largest, and its headquarters were at The Angel and the George and Dragon. The latter also hosted a rowing club. While some cyclists enjoyed the bumps and spills of the rough roads, most required the potholes to be filled. To keep the roadmen sweet, especially on the notorious Portsmouth Road, the cycling association of Thames Ditton treated them to a sumptuous meal at the George and Dragon or The Angel.

Incidentally, as I was leaving the inn I noticed the strangest of structures. It appeared to be a shed in an alarming state of disrepair. It was shaped like an inverted pyramid and bore a notice warning not to stand or sit underneath the structure. You are preaching to the converted, old mate.

RICHMOND: *PRINCE'S HEAD*

The Prince's Head is on The Green, which is bounded by George Street,
Twickenham Road (A316) and the River Thames.

Volumes have been written about Richmond Palace. Of the amazing building
constructed by kings Edward I and Edward II only a gateway and the wardrobe
court (which once housed between 2,000 and 3,000 of Queen Elizabeth I's dresses)
now remain, the palace having been demolished in 1648. Its golden age was the
time of Queen Elizabeth I. She was born and died by the river. The surviving
gatehouse is said to be the place where her ring was thrown after her death to a
waiting horseman. His duty was to ride with it, post-haste, to inform James VI of
Scotland.

On the green, close to where the palace stood, now stands the Prince's Head. On a
warm day the green is packed with potential customers. Thirsty patrons swarm the
tables of this pub and of the Cricketers next door. This is another tardis pub, far more

spacious than its external appearance
would suggest. There are large rooms
and sizeable alcoves. The walls are
adorned by photographs of the green,
cricketers, the Thames and teams of
rowers.

There is little to surprise in the
history of the inn, which was built in
1740. A famous landlord in the late
1800s was W.G. East, a very famous
sculler. Later, Tom Richardson took
over; he played cricket for Surrey,
taking 1,005 wickets in four seasons.
In the early 1900s the Prince's Head
had a reputation for trouble. A bar
was divided off for the exclusive use of
ladies, who otherwise could not enter
unless in the company of a gentleman. All has now changed.

The unique name of the Prince's
Head deserves comment. Kings,
Queens and Dukes we have in
abundance, but apparently only one
Prince's Head. A notice on the wall
suggests that it makes reference to
the famous Prince of Wales, or possibly to Charles I, who lost his head.

RICHMOND HILL: *THE ROEBUCK*

Richmond Hill is the B321. It leaves the A307 at Star and Garter Hill.
The Roebuck is No. 130.

This appears to be a rather small pub, perhaps because it is dwarfed by its surroundings. It struggles between such grandiose neighbours as the Richmond Gate Hotel and the Richmond Hill Hotel. Opposite it are houses such as The Wick and Wick House. In the early to mid-eighteenth century a wealthy female socialite

gave parties here that were extremely daring for the time. But all passed in the fullness of time: 'Golden lads and ladies must like chimney sweepers come to dust.'

Alexander Pope, the eccentric poet, had a house near to The Roebuck, and in his garden he nurtured the oldest weeping willow in Europe. The view from the front of The Roebuck is magnificent. Arthur Mee, the writer and producer of many county histories, states: 'If we count Richmond as part of London then this is the noblest view that London can command.'

It certainly is expansive, stretching from nearby Petersham Meadow with its mysteriously enchanting Gothic-towered hotel to the Berkshire hills and even the ridge of the Hog's Back between Guildford and Farnham. A nearby board points out places of interest for the uninformed. Windsor Castle, Hampton Court, the ruins of Richmond Castle and Ham House may be detected in this panoramic delight. However, a clear, mistless day is needed to make out these cornerstones of history and culture.

It would be superfluous to list the names of those famous people who have found the terrace outside The Roebuck a great enticement. Suffice it to say that, among them, Joshua Reynolds returned time and time again, Turner spent hours here, painting, and Sir Walter Scott found it highly inspirational.

The inside of the Roebuck is a little ordinary. However, it does have a spook, one strong enough to have sent a couple of CID officers scrambling out of the bedroom in which it had been their intention to stay the night.

RICHMOND: *HOLE IN THE WALL*

The Hole in the Wall is on Park Road, which runs between Friars Style Road (B322) and Queens Road (B353).

This little inn, sitting above the town of Richmond, has a grim story to tell. In fact, they do not come much grimmer than this. With the possible exception of Elizabeth Dyer, the 'baby farmer' whom we met in Reading, Kate Webster was the most loathed woman of Victorian times.

Kate arrived in Liverpool from Ireland in 1849. She meandered from job to job, man to man and prison to prison. The only person to whom Kate ever showed any love, respect or loyalty was her tiny illegitimate son Johnie. Kate arrived in superior Richmond with Johnie in 1879. She found employment as a housemaid and skivvy with Mrs Julia Thompson, a respectable middle-aged widow living in Park Road.

Their relationship became a coexistence that verged on a cold war. Mrs Thompson was pernickety, fastidious and meticulous to a fault. Kate was slapdash and slovenly, with a foul and easily erupting temper. It soon became apparent, through hints dropped to friends, that Julia Thompson was in constant fear of personal violence or worse.

To cut a long story short, Kate killed her mistress with a meat axe, boiled and roasted the dissected body, threw the head over Hammersmith Bridge and placed the remainder of the corpse in a trunk. She then engaged an unsuspecting boy to push the trunk, on a trolley, further down the river and deposit it, where subsequently it was washed up. Kate sold her mistress's clothes and adorned herself in her mistress's jewellery.

She then attempted to sell some pots of dripping to the landlord of the Hole in the Wall. You've guessed it – Kate Webster was not a woman who wasted anything. Whether or not the landlord took advantage of the offer, we do not know.

Kate seemed to be begging to be caught, and caught she was. Selling Mrs Thompson's furniture and load-ing it into two large conveyances

The execution of
Kate Webster.
(*Author's collection*)

were hardly conducive to covering up the crime. Already worried neighbours became alarmed and called the police.

Kate fled to Ireland with Johnie, but it took no time for the authorities to trace and extradite her. She was convicted, and hanged at Wandsworth on 30 July 1879. The penny dreadfuls had a field day; the story had everything to entice the avid reader. So there we have it, a horrendous story, and such a pleasant little pub.

RICHMOND: *LASS O' RICHMOND HILL*

The A305 becomes Sheen Road in Richmond. Opposite Manor Road turn right into Queens Road, the B353. The Lass o' Richmond Hill is not far up on the right.

This is as near to a perfect pub as one can get. The views from the Hill are stupendous. The pub itself is attractive, both inside and out. The interior is vast, and has many interesting features. Hundreds of empty wine bottles adorn almost every horizontal surface. This is both unusual and attractive, each window sill – of which there are many – having its regimented line of bottles. Other attractions include pictures showing early nineteenth-century needlepoint embroidery and massive, ancient beams expounding wise and moral quotations such as 'Poor and content is rich enough', 'Call frequently, drink moderately, leave friendly'. All very good advice.

As I sat one fine spring morning in the back bar – reserved for smokers and other outcasts – I wondered why some pubs embellish their surroundings with musty old dead hops. They are not the most becoming of sights and I always reflect on the waste. Why weren't they lovingly crushed in their youth to make a tankard of fine ale?

This inn is obviously named after the beautiful 'Lass of Richmond Hill' – an ancient song. Who composed the words and music is not known. However, it is commonly agreed that the lass was a beautiful maiden, possibly a barmaid, and that she used her looks to become very rich in a very short period of time. What is a matter of quite heated debate is the location of the sweet lass's rise to comfortable affluence.

Was she from Richmond, Yorkshire, or Richmond, Surrey?

Over the years neither town would concede, but it appears that they have now agreed to disagree. Earlier, each town produced a faded and yellowing manuscript on which only a few of the words could be discerned. Those that could be read differed to a degree. In the Surrey version, after a lot of 'tum-tis' and 'rumpti-tums', the lass of Richmond Hill says 'I will'. Later on, after several more 'umpti-tums', we hear:

> Which wasn't to her credit
> But when she tum-ti tum-ti tum
> She wished she hadn't said it.

Less respectful, but more fun, is the Yorkshire version. After a similar number of 'umpti, tumpti tums', the song ends with:

> But when she umpti diddly dee
> It didn't affect her heart
> So what the umpti called her was
> The Ilkley Moor bar tart.

Well, wherever you come from, 'Lass', you have a fine pub named after you in Richmond, Surrey.

TWICKENHAM: *POPE'S GROTTO*

In the centre of Twickenham, the Staines Road (A305) becomes King Street. Follow the signs to the A310. You are immediately in Cross Deep. The Pope's Grotto is a short distance on your right.

Pope's Grotto overlooks the Thames and Radnor Gardens. It is within easy reach of the world-famous rugby ground and not far from Strawberry Hill, Horace Walpole's brave and eccentric adventure into Gothic revival. Perhaps those possessed of a more orderly taste should take a stroll to Marble Hill House. This beautifully restored Palladian villa was built by George II for his mistress, Henrietta Howard. Very little is known about the history of Pope's Grotto. Although far younger than its namesake, it is named after Alexander Pope, the well-known poet. Pope had a villa here, and could often be seen strolling with his bosom friends, Gay, Swift and

Arbuthnot. They would compose poems and philosophise, while skimming stones across the water.

Pope's Grotto is now a hotel, and has been extended on several occasions. The bars have an easy-going atmosphere, and, in spite of the establishment's hotel status, they still evoke a type of village-inn flavour. Having the ambience of a 'local' in no way detracts from the refined and sophisticated overall setting. Sitting under a canopy of trees in the gardens and watching the youthful couples stroll by, silhouetted against the vast open sky, is a 'must' for old romantics.

I wonder whether Pope was gazing on this expanse as he toyed with thoughts of life elsewhere among the enticing stars. I think it probable that he penned these immortal lines while sitting by the Thames at Twickenham:

> Who sees with equal eye, as God of all,
> A hero perish, or a sparrow fall
> Atoms and systems into ruin hurl'd
> And now a bubble burst, and now a world.

ISLEWORTH: *LONDON APPRENTICE*

In Isleworth, Richmond Road (A300) becomes South Street. At this point the tiny Swan Street leads off it into Church Street, home of the London Apprentice.

The London Apprentice is probably one of the best-known pubs in the country, its attractive exterior having been the subject of innumerable paintings. Seldom has a book on pubs been produced without the London Apprentice taking pride of place.

In the not too distant past it was the custom to apprentice a renegade son to one of the city companies. To keep the hot-blooded young men on a tight rein they were limited to one day's holiday a year. On this day the apprentices headed out of the city to the nearby villages. Isleworth was one such village, where they would indulge their pent-up riotous behaviour. Hence the name of this village tavern.

As the London Apprentice stands on the waterfront, it was connected with the smuggling trade. It is said that a tunnel still exists. Personally, I am sceptical. Usually,

what are thought to be tunnels are actually the long cellars that were built to keep the beer cool. It is said that Henry VIII and Lady Jane Grey courted here in the inn's early days. The evidence would seem to be far stronger that Charles Dickens was a regular at the London Apprentice. Here he would meet Wilkie Collins, and several others of his fellow authors.

There is also a ghost here, but that is a subject for some future discussion.

Charles Dickens.
(Illustrated London News)

STRAND ON THE GREEN: *BULL'S HEAD*

The Bull's Head is in Thames Street, which runs parallel with the river.

This is another lovely old Thames-side inn. The Bull's Head is over 350 years old. It has elegantly swallowed up a row of nearby cottages, and is now much enlarged.

The atmosphere of the Bull's Head is enchanting. Beamed and half-panelled nooks and crannies lead off in all directions. I have heard it described as 'tranquil, low-ceilinged and charming'. I can vouch for the charming, a bump on the head is evidence of the low ceiling, but the inn was hardly tranquil when I arrived at lunchtime. There were diners everywhere.

I took my pint outside and looked across from the Thames towpath to Oliver's Eyot – Oliver being Cromwell, of course. His daughter Mary, the Countess Fauconberg, lived nearby. The story goes that, during the Civil War, Cromwell and some of his closest associates were resting at the inn. The puritan Cromwell was an abstainer, but some of his companions imbibed a little. The group's relaxation was rudely interrupted by a barmaid's shouting that a troop of

Royalists was approaching. The landlord, being a man of presence of mind, led the party down to his cellar and smuggled his companions, by means of a subterranean passage, to a small island on the Thames. There the men lay until the danger subsided. The island was subsequently renamed Oliver's Eyot.

As I gazed across the 20 yards or so to this mud heap, I wondered who on earth would want to dig a subterranean passage to it. It would have cost a fortune to construct, and for what purpose? Who would want to visit a hump of mud? I do wonder why the Royalists did not search such a close and probable hiding place.

LONDON, SW13: *YE WHITE HART*

Ye White Hart is on The Terrace, the B350, beside the river and close to Barnes Bridge station.

My first visit to this beautiful old riverside pub was in late October 2004. A massive advertisement decorating one of the walls announced: 'Best view of fireworks on the river.' I did not doubt it for one minute. There are delightful views

of the Thames from the terrace of this many-storeyed old inn, and by this point in the Thames there are views of the annual university boat race.

A plaque at Ye White Hart informs us that the building was there as early as 1662 – making it one of the oldest pubs on the river. It is mentioned in 1676, when it was named the King's Arms. The proprietor was then one Robert Warner, who passed the licence on to his son Charles (information from Peter Haydon). The licence remained in the Warner family until 1736. By 1776 an affluent local family named Trewy were the proprietors and the 'Ye White Hart' board was above the door.

In the 1890s Ye White Hart was extensively rebuilt, giving the inn a delightful Victorian character. The rebuilding work probably also accounts for the extension, with its unusual flat roof.

Once again, there is an absence of colourful stories, but Ye White Hart's location and ambience make it a 'must' for a visit.

LONDON, SW15: *DUKE'S HEAD*

Cross Barnes Common from west to east; the Duke's Head is near the embankment, on Lower Richmond Road, the B349.

Here is Victorian pub architecture at its best. The Duke's Head was built in 1832, rebuilt, for some unknown reason, in 1864, and altered yet again in 1894. The views across the river from the Duke's Head are splendid. It is close to Putney Bridge and, of course, the start of the university boat race. Don't even attempt to get near the bar on boat-race day.

This is one of those old inns that one knows must have been the location for a hundred colourful stories, none of which has been recorded for posterity.

Peter Haydon, in *The London Pub*, tells us that the Duke's Head was a victim of the 'island bar', an invention of Isambard Kingdom Brunel. At large railway stations, such as Swindon and Crewe, great numbers of people would wait to change trains. Where else would one want to wait, but in a bar? Large as the bars were, they were inadequate to cope with the volume of trade. Therefore a number of small bars would be opened under one roof. They were more efficient and more personal, and the many alcoves were more private for young lovers.

The railway bars soon spread to the river, and the vast floor space of the Duke's Head did not exempt it from the new development. Unfortunately, the smaller bars encouraged not only young lovers but also pickpockets and prostitutes. The magistrates did all they could to discourage them, and, in time, most pubs returned to their original large bars. Personally, I am glad they did, for eating in the capacious dining room of the Duke's Head, with its view of the river on three sides, is an experience not be missed.

LONDON, W6: *THE DOVE*

The Dove is in Upper Mall, a continuation of Lower Mall.

The Dove is an extremely attractive and famous little hostelry. It has a colourful history and is justifiably proud of its status as a historical monument. It even holds a certificate to prove it.

It is approached down a short and narrow alleyway, an alley once famed for duels and for the reputed duellist's command, 'Landlord, bring me two pistols and one bottle of champagne'.

The inn's terrace overlooks the river and is an ideal viewpoint during the university boat race. However, it is not difficult to imagine the scene in olden days, when swarthy watermen landed barges here, loaded with goods for the capital. I had not been inside The Dove for fifteen years when I visited it in 2005. I was quickly reminded of the low beams when I saw a barmaid a little more than five feet tall duck her head. Nothing has changed; the place is still in semi-darkness, and still has its low beams, panelled walls and wooden floors. The deep cellars remain too, as do the fine prints and ancient fireplaces. The ambience is intact, as when Charles I toasted Nell Gwynne here.

The public room is cramped. In the bar – arguably the smallest in England – is a plaque showing a menacingly high watermark dated 1928. It must have been a worrying time on the Thames.

The Dove has played host to many celebrities over the centuries. Peter Haydon, in his excellent book *The London Pub*, informs us that the composer Khachaturian and novelists Graham Greene and Ernest Hemingway were regular patrons, as were Richard Burton and fellow thespian Rex Harrison.

Numerous other celebrities who have enjoyed a drink at The Dove include the English painter Frank Brangwyn, who fell in love with the inn after visiting his friend William Morris, who lived next door. Turner sat here to paint his orange sunsets. The artists jostled with authors: Thomas Burke penned his popular books on London scenes here, and the pub named The Pigeon in Sir Alan Herbert's *The Water Gypsies* is probably The Dove. George Izzard, one-time landlord, wrote 'One for the Road' here, and Frank Thompson rested at The Dove while writing his famous poem 'The Seasons'. There was no shortage of royalty among the inn's customers. The Duke of Sussex, Queen Victoria's uncle, tried to retire to a house next door so that he could just toddle round for a social drink – an ambition that was doomed to failure. The fame and popularity of the man assured a large, if unwanted, entourage that quickly engulfed the small building.

To end on a sad note, one celebrity regular not yet mentioned was James Thomson, the genius who gave us 'Rule Britannia'. Thomson's love of the place brought about his downfall. He died of a fever brought on by inclement weather when he insisted on crossing the Thames in an open boat during a downpour. His mission – to drink at his beloved Dove.

LONDON, W6: *BLACK LION*

The Black Lion can be found on the corner of Lower Mall and Black Lion Lane.

The Black Lion is one of six attractive pubs standing on Hammersmith's stretch of the river. Its towering white façade looks majestically over the Thames and is surrounded by a sea of millionaires' abodes. Every dwelling in this area seems to be adorned with a blue plaque stating that some great philosopher, writer, artist or statesman dwelt within its walls. The Black Lion has a plaque of its own.

The inn was closed when I last called, but, thankfully, I am told that this is not a permanent situation. I had to content myself with strolling in the garden before descending the fifteen white steps to the strand. Hopefully, little has changed inside. I recall a long, narrow bar room with picturesque old pictures of the Thames on the walls, and one of the few skittle alleys in London. The Black Lion's plaque, or, to be more accurate, its noticeboard, informs the reader of an interesting history. Just over 200 years ago the Black Lion was the home of a pig farmer who brewed beer in his spare time. The demand for ale soon outstripped the call for bacon, and so the Black Lion was born.

One could not leave the Black Lion without mentioning the famous Hammersmith ghost – who was not really a ghost at all. Briefly, this is the story.

The Hammersmith ghost.

In the winter of 1804 a frightening spectre was reported several times in Hammersmith village. A tall white ghost terrified onlookers as it made its way from nearby St Paul's Church to the riverside by the Black Lion. Alarm spread among the locals, and an unsubstantiated report said that one poor woman died of fright. The residents of the village had had enough. A group of excise men and other stalwarts formed a vigilante team to lie in wait each night, armed with blunderbusses and an assortment of improvised weapons.

On the fourth night a ghostly white figure appeared. A trigger-happy excise officer named Francis Smith panicked and fired his weapon. The figure in white fell to the ground. Upon investigation, the vigilantes found the dying man to be Thomas Milwood, a plasterer returning from night work, still clad in his lime-soaked overalls. He was carried swiftly to the Black Lion, where he soon expired.

A true and sad little story.

LONDON, W6: *BLUE ANCHOR*

The Blue Anchor can be found just south of the Great West Road (A4). Coming from the west, turn right shortly before the Hammersmith flyover into Lower Mall.

To sit outside the Blue Anchor at one of the many tables on a sunny day is a most satisfying experience. The view is delightful, and the variety of customers is interesting in the extreme. It has been since 1722, and long may it remain so.

It is worth taking a short stroll from the Blue Anchor to Hammersmith Bridge. The first suspension bridge was constructed between 1824 and 1827, but the splendid, eye-catching structure one sees today was the brainchild of Joseph Bazalgette, the genius of London's drainage construction, who was knighted in 1874. Bazalgette's structure, built between 1883 and 1887, is arguably the most attractive bridge on the Thames and well worth a visit. On the other side of the bridge, in Barnes, is an interesting wildlife reserve, the London Wetland Centre. Back over the bridge, take a walk westwards to Fuller's Brewery and Chiswick House, the home of Lord Burlington of Royal Academy fame.

Inside the pub one is struck by the smallness of the interior – hence, no doubt, the collection of outside seats. The Blue Anchor is a rowing pub (not surprising, given that it is situated roughly midway between Putney and Mortlake, the university boat-race course), and it has more the atmosphere of a private rowing club than that of a pub. Blades, oars and other similar paraphernalia adorn the walls and are suspended from the ceiling. A very varied collection of prints hangs on the panelled walls.

The Blue Anchor's most famous regular was Gustav Holst, probably best known for his *Planets* suite, written between 1914 and 1916. Holst became director of music at St Paul's Girls' School in nearby Brook Green and it was his wont to drop in

regularly, mostly alone, but occasionally with his friend and fellow composer Vaughan Williams. According to information provided by the inn, this was the location that inspired Holst's *Hammersmith* suite, which he composed while seated at a table and watching the Thames.

I have a feeling that the old master would find the Blue Anchor little changed if he returned today. There was always the rowing interest – an interest brought to the fore when it was used as a location in a film called *Sliding Doors* starring John Hannah and Gwyneth Paltrow. One could easily laze away the day here but at least another half-dozen historic inns lie within easy walking distance. However, before leaving, give yourself time to inspect and to enquire about the antique beer engine, a very rare machine indeed.

LONDON, SW18: *THE ALMA*

The Alma is opposite Wandsworth station, in Old York Road.

The Alma is difficult to find because of road alterations, and it was only after some effort that I discovered it opposite Wandsworth station. The Alma is named after some cottages, which in turn were named after the nearby Alma Road. Obviously

the road was called after the Crimea battle. In 1854, 26,000 English and French troops under Lord Raglan and Marshal St Arnaud dislodged 40,000 Russian troops from the heights above the Alma River. Celebrations followed and many pubs gloried in the name. The Alma at Wandsworth was built twelve years later in 1866, when the euphoria had waned a little but was still in existence.

The Alma of today has been modified a little but still has the charm inherent with a type of Gallic romance. There is definitely a French atmosphere here. It is probably due to the large open lounge with its four-sided bar, the likes of which can be seen from Calais to Perpignan. There are some fine painted mirrors here, and I am indebted to Peter Haydon for informing me of the rustic dining table of immense proportions and the decorative plaster frieze discovered during alterations.

I seldom mention pub conveniences, but I must just remark upon those at The Alma. They are way below in the cellars and next to the Gents is an intriguing niche of a room containing champagne and other wines. An ornamental steel door precludes one from entry. On entering the toilet one's eye is drawn to the washbasins. They are old domestic sinks, the type your gran washed up in, and the sort of item that now fetches a fortune at garden centres.

I must also mention the signboard. It depicts a scene presumably from the Alma battle. A cannon has been fired by British troops and where the cannonball should be there is a circular hole.

I thought it was whimsical.

LONDON, SW18: *THE SHIP*

The Ship is in Jews Road in Wandsworth. Jews Road is a tiny street forking off the A217 south of the Thames, immediately before Wandsworth Bridge.

My thirty-year-old map book of London was little help in finding Jews Row. In fact I was about to give up after crossing and recrossing Wandsworth Bridge three times and circulating a massive roundabout on a similar number of occasions. I finally found it up a tiny road just at the foot of the bridge. Unfortunately for The Ship, a cement works has opened up next door, hardly conducive to trade.

This is a Young's pub, which is always a recommendation. It is also a summer pub where people may sit outside at tables and watch the old Thames waltz idly by. The Ship originated in 1809. In the early days it was not quite on the strand, for it was separated from the riverbank by a line of cottages. The brewery obtained the buildings in 1848 and promptly knocked them down, thereby making easy access to the Thames. In the late 1980s the conservatory was added. It is used for dining, and is a mecca for the owners of the exclusive apartments that are mushrooming nearby.

I arrived at noon on a very wet and windy January day. I stayed in the bar; it was old, plain, adequate, practical and thoroughly clean throughout. An old harmonium

is still there. On the stairs I noticed a picture of a gentleman dressed in a ballerina's tutu. Underneath is inscribed 'Presented in 1983'. I would love to know the story.

'Scooterman' advertises at the inn. Apparently if you have had too much to drink, Scooterman will arrive on his minute vehicle. He will fold it up, put it in your boot and then proceed to drive you home in your car, obviously at a price. When he has delivered his customer, he removes his scooter from the boot and rides off into the sunset to await another call. Who said private enterprise is dead.

LONDON, SW1: *RED LION*

The Red Lion is north of the river, on the corner of Derby Gate and Parliament Street, which runs north of Parliament Square.

This is a wonderful old West End pub that is situated on the corner of Parliament Street and Derby Gate. It is long and narrow with a bar that seems to run from one end to the other.

One of several busts in the establishment is that of Geoffrey Chaucer. The pub is old – reputedly it has been around in some form since 1437 – but it is too young for Chaucer, who shuffled off this mortal coil in 1400. There is also a bust of Dickens, who was far more familiar with the Red Lion and used it as the inn in *David Copperfield*. Other famous names associated with the inn are William Kent, Sir John Soane and Sir Charles Barry, three of the country's most renowned architects who designed the Treasury opposite. One would imagine that there was much celebration at the Red Lion when the magnificent building was completed in 1845.

The Red Lion also had several more celebrated neighbours. A few steps down lived Sir George Burke, a great friend of Isambard Kingdom Brunel. At one time the intrepid engineer lodged opposite. The two fixed a string and bell across the street so that they could attract one another's attention: possibly not one of Brunel's greatest engineering feats.

At the end of the long bar there is a short flight of stairs to an upper dining room. It was here that the Labour modernisers met to create New Labour in the early 1990s. The close proximity of Parliament would make the Red Lion popular among politicians. One wonders what political intrigue and scheming have taken place here over the centuries. If those walls could only speak!

But it gets worse. When the police resided in Scotland Yard, the Red Lion was their natural watering hole. What plans and manipulations were hatched here? What traps were baited and sprung?

Police and politicians rubbing shoulders! Skulduggery is too soft a word.

LONDON, WC2: *SHERLOCK HOLMES*

The Sherlock Homes is in Northumberland Street, which leads off the Strand.

Although not strictly speaking on the Thames, the Sherlock Holmes is just a few steps away, so, despite massive coverage already, I found it impossible to exclude from this collection. In the days when I could afford to stay in the Charing Cross

Hotel, the Sherlock Holmes, the Ship and Shovell and the Coal Hole were the first three places I visited.

Every flat surface and nearly every breathing space is full of artefacts and memorabilia of Conan Doyle's world-famous hero. Whitbreads acquired the collection in 1957 after the winding-up of the Festival of Britain in 1951. Other exhibits were contributed by descendants of Sir Arthur himself.

I remember my first visit in 1964 when there were fewer exhibits. A plastered Holmes – that is, a plaster statue of Holmes – was there, complete with deerstalker hat. The eyes of the Baskerville hound stared down menacingly – a most disturbing experience, which was in no way diluted by the stuffed 'speckled band' cobra coiled within striking distance. It was a bit of luck that Watson's service revolver

was close at hand. There are now many more exhibits, as new films provide extra material. The Sherlock Holmes, once Northumberland Arms, is aptly situated. It is beside and part of the Old Northumberland Hotel. Conan Doyle, reputedly a regular, used it as the London retreat of Sir Henry Baskerville when he was in fear of the heinous hound, and it was here that the master sleuth traced Francis Hay Moulton in 'The Adventure of the Noble Bachelor'. The Turkish baths Holmes frequented were adjacent to the hotel.

Thanks to more recent developments, Holmes's study can be seen through a glass partition from the restaurant and also from the roof garden. I have had many a drink and several meals in the Sherlock Holmes; it has always been a pleasurable experience and I look forward to many more.

LONDON, EC4: *BLACK FRIAR*

The Black Friar stands at the junction of Queen Victoria Street and New Bridge Street, close to Blackfriars station.

I wish I had a photograph of the interior of the Black Friar, but when I was inside I didn't have a camera and when I had a camera the pub wasn't open.

Now dwarfed by surrounding buildings, the Black Friar looks a little like an interloper. The exterior, however, is whimsically capricious: it reminds one of a wedge of cheese between several massive slices of bread, and it is adorned by a large plaster Dominican friar. Although the building is relatively young (1902–4), a Dominican friary stood here from 1279 until the Reformation in 1539. A licensed hostelry has been on the site for some 350 years. We are reliably informed that this is the place where the Holy Roman Emperor Charles V, the Papal Magistrate and Henry VIII all met in 1532. The subject under discussion was the dissolution of Henry's marriage to Catherine of Aragon.

Internally, the Anglicised art nouveau was criticised by the Arts and Crafts Movement as being the most outstandingly eccentric in London. At the narrow end of

the building a mock baronial hall leads to a room lavish and difficult to analyse. Friezes in copper and plaster by Henry Poole depict jolly monks by the dozen in various heights of revelry. There would seem to be a consensus of agreed indulgence. The atmosphere is pleasing here if just a trifle bizarre. An opulent marble-pillared inglenook fireplace, gleaming mirrors and a low vaulted mosaic ceiling add to the eccentric charm of the place. I am informed that subtle opium-smoking hints are modelled in the embellishment of the fireplace. If so, they have eluded me. More obvious, in fact blatantly so, are some scattered pearls of wisdom that seem to tell the celebrating brothers that everything has its price, so please indulge in moderation, if that is not a contradiction in terms.

I quote: 'Finery is foolery'; 'Silence is golden'; 'Haste is slow'; 'Industry is all' and my favourite, 'Don't advertise, tell a gossip'.

I shall definitely return to the Black Friar.

LONDON, SE1: *MARKET PORTER*

Market Porter is in Stoney Street, which is an extension of Bankside. This leads into Southwark Bridge Road, which is the A300, running south from Southwark Bridge.

The Market Porter is arguably the best real-ale pub in London. It has been around since 1638 and was probably one of the many merry hostelries that set up in Borough High Street when the old bridge was the only crossing into the city. It is

very close to Southwark Cathedral and the Old Hop Exchange. If pubs had celebrity status, the Market Porter would be at the forefront. Famous actors are inclined to drop in when working in Park Street. The whole area is a ready-made set for any Dickensian production.

Close by in Clink Street is the Old Thameside. Once described as a good pastiche of ancient taverns, this two-storey building is festooned with candles, old beams, flagstones, timbers and pews. It also has spectacular views of the river.

Also nearby at Bankside is the world-famous Anchor. It has been recently reopened after extensive modernisation and enlargement. A large Premier Hotel now adorns the one-time car park. The Anchor is saturated with history. It was here that Samuel Pepys witnessed the formidable destruction of the Great Fire of London in 1666. The Anchor suffered greatly in the fire and was rebuilt in 1676. Dr Johnson was a regular here (where wasn't he?), as were many celebrities over the centuries. This is film country and just to show that the notable dignitaries are not all in the past Tom Cruise looked in for a pint during the filming of *Mission Impossible*.

LONDON, SE1: *GEORGE INN*

George Inn is at the northern end of Borough High Street, just over London Bridge and close to Southwark Cathedral.

It is just a short walk from the Market Porter to The George. Once the George and Dragon, this lovely old pub in historic Southwark is the capital's last remaining galleried inn. Chaucer's Tabard has sadly gone, as have countless others that adorned the Borough High Street. The Tabard, the meeting place of the Canterbury pilgrims, disappeared in 1875; it was far too ripe for redevelopment for it to survive. But The George is owned by the National Trust, which should ensure its survival.

There are records of a tavern on this site as early as 1554. It is just south of London Bridge, near what was Traitors Gate. I wonder if the sight of defectors' and felons' heads stuck on spikes was conducive to the quaffing of ale. Southwark was just outside the city's gates, which made it immune from the capital's laws – hence the abundance of the bullrings, bear-baiting pits, theatres and brothels for which it was famous.

The George was fully established in King Henry VIII's reign. According to Peter Haydon's book *The London Pub*, the first recorded landlord in 1558 was a Nicholas Marten. Having survived the Great Fire of London intact, The George was partially destroyed in 1670 by a fire that started in its rope store. A further fire in 1676 destroyed the building completely along with some 500 other buildings. It was rebuilt in 1677, when the galleried section was extended to three sides.

Shakespeare, who managed the nearby Globe Theatre, was a regular at The George. There is a story, by no means substantiated, that a saucy barmaid jokingly took his key to the Globe and placed it between her ample breasts together with the

key to her bedroom. She then enquired of the Bard which key he desired. His answer is not recorded.

Incidentally, Edmund Shakespeare (player/actor) and reputedly brother of William, was buried at the nearby Cathedral Church of St Saviour in 1607. No doubt Edmund trod the boards in The George's courtyard.

No ancient London inn would be complete without a visit from Dickens. The George is no exception. The famous novelist used the inn in *Little Dorrit*; it is the hostelry that Tip visits. Quite as prolific in visiting alehouses was Dr Johnson. The famous critic, essayist and lexicographer had a friend named Thrale who owned a brewery at Streatham (I wish I had). Johnson and Thrale would stop the coach at The George and indulge for several hours; those were the days.

I first visited The George in the early 1960s. I remember a wealth of old wooden panelling and being served by buxom wenches in seventeenth-century attire. In those days local actors performed on a cart in the courtyard, usually on Shakespeare day, 23 April. An Egon Ronay directory of the early 1960s is full of praise for the culinary services of The George. It describes mouth-watering prawn cock-tails and gargantuan steak and kidney pies. But at 4s 6d a portion, one has to heed one's pocket.

LONDON, SE16: *THE ANGEL*

The Angel is in Bermondsey Wall East. South of the river at Tower Bridge, head east on the A200, Jamaica Road. Opposite Southwark Park, turn left into Cathay Street, which becomes Bermondsey Wall East.

The Angel stands alone. Its nearest neighbours are a block of flats and a ruined manor that belonged to Edward III in 1350.

There has been some type of watering hole here since the fifteenth century, obviously supplying sustenance to pilgrims visiting the monks of Bermondsey who dwelt in the adjacent priory. The present building is Georgian, dating only from the nineteenth century, but in no way does this detract from the site's rich history.

In its early days The Angel was known as the Salvation Inn. It was here in 1820 that Captain Jones hired a crew for his pilgrim's trip to New England (see The Mayflower). The inn was also used as a recruiting office by the famous Captain James Cook before he sailed for Australia in 1768.

One famous patron of The Angel was Samuel Johnson. He is said to have written for the exclusive *Gentleman's Magazine* here. It is to be wondered how this famous lexicographer reconciled his genteel observations while rubbing shoulders with the thieves, murderers, fraudsters, wardens from the Clink, pickpockets and smugglers who certainly frequented this abode. Incidentally there is a trapdoor in the building that is thought to have been used by smugglers.

The inn could also have been used in assisting the escape of locals from the notorious press gangs that roamed this part of the Thames.

Another patron of The Angel was Samuel Pepys, who found the inn a pleasant country walk from the city. Obviously this was a goodly time before the docks and warehouses. However, Pepys could have been enticed here by some fringe benefits, as a little-known story suggests. Perhaps Pepys was a little less moralistic than might have been supposed. The famous diarist mentions watching a certain Mrs Bagwell from the inn as she hung her clean washing. Pepys later 'enjoyed the lady's company' on many occasions. For some obscure reason Samuel always had a slight guilty conscience when he left the lady. He remedied this situation by purchasing some cherries for his wife in the nearby Cherry Garden. Whether it was the tiring walk back to the city or the strain of 'conversation' with Mrs Bagwell is not known, but Pepys often needed sustenance on his journey home and so scoffed the aforementioned cherries. Then his returning conscience dictated that he buy his wife a new hat. What a fine collection of headwear Mrs Pepys must have possessed.

Internally, The Angel has one large bar. Its walls are decorated with prints of old ships. Unfortunately the side door that leads to the balcony was closed awaiting repair when I was there. However, spectacular views from London Bridge to St Paul's can be enjoyed from the establishment.

ROTHERHITHE: *THE MAYFLOWER*

Continue along Jamaica Road, over the roundabout, into Brunel Road. The Mayflower is in Rotherhithe Street, which runs parallel. There are several turnings left linking the roads.

Another attractive old pub is The Mayflower, dwarfed between warehouses that have been reincarnated into unaffordable flats.

Little has changed at The Mayflower over the years. Obviously it still has its wooden jetty supported by heavy piles to stop it meeting a watery grave. Also it still has the fetching black-and-white façade with its latticed windows.

The Mayflower dates from 1600, but most of the present building arrived some 200 years later. It was originally named the Spread Eagle and Crown or The Shippe, or possibly both over the centuries. The name of Mayflower is relatively new. It appeared in 1957 as a somewhat delayed appreciation of the Pilgrim Fathers.

The Mayflower is unique in pub history for at one time acting as a post office. It sold stamps, so that sailors who were only briefly ashore could send letters to their loved ones. The practice has long since ceased, but I am told that USA stamps may still be purchased here.

Other than having most of its upper floor destroyed in the Blitz, The Mayflower's main claim to historical fame is the Pilgrim Fathers.

In 1620 Captain Christopher Jones, part-owner of the *Mayflower*, departed from Rotherhithe (not Plymouth) in his 180-ton ship for New England. He survived the perilous ordeal, only to return to England in 1621 and die shortly afterwards. Captain Jones is buried in the nearby St Mary the Virgin's churchyard.

Careful examination reveals that a certain amount of restoration has been discreetly carried out, but the atmosphere is 100 per cent genuine: the darkened ceiling with beams, the panelled walls and the unique old settle seats inscribed with wisdom. Inevitably memorabilia from the original Mayflower abound. There are also some wonderful old prints of Rotherhithe.

It would be easy to spend many hours here just quaffing booze and drinking in the atmosphere. But there is an exhibition of the steam engine that was used on the Rotherhithe tunnel just across the way.

LONDON, E1: *PROSPECT OF WHITBY*

The Prospect of Whitby is in Wapping Wall. Returning north of the river, head east from Tower Bridge along the A1203, The Highway. After half a mile or so, turn right into Garnet Street or Glamis Road to reach Wapping Wall.

The funnels and masts are long gone, as have the attractively ugly warehouses, boatyards and cranes. But the Prospect of Whitby, reputedly the oldest pub on the river, remains, albeit sandwiched between two massive blocks of flats.

It was an adventure for a teenager like myself, in the 1960s, to visit this charming old London pub. I remember well the conglomeration of artefacts inside: skulls, bottles, pistols and nautical bric-a-brac of every description. If my memory serves me right, there was even an upright Victorian musical box. What an atmosphere.

The charm and atmosphere are still here, but the characters and camaraderie have gone. Patrons are now tourists and flat-dwellers rather than the lightermen and dockers who sustained the inn for centuries.

The Prospect of Whitby (I have diligently tried to trace the origin of the name but with no success; I can only assume that many boats sailed from here to the Yorkshire port) originated in 1520 during the reign of Henry VIII. The bow-windowed dining room once commemorated Samuel Pepys. The acclaimed diarist was a regular here, and it has been suggested that some of the raucous seafaring company contributed to many of the seamier incidents that Pepys recorded. In its

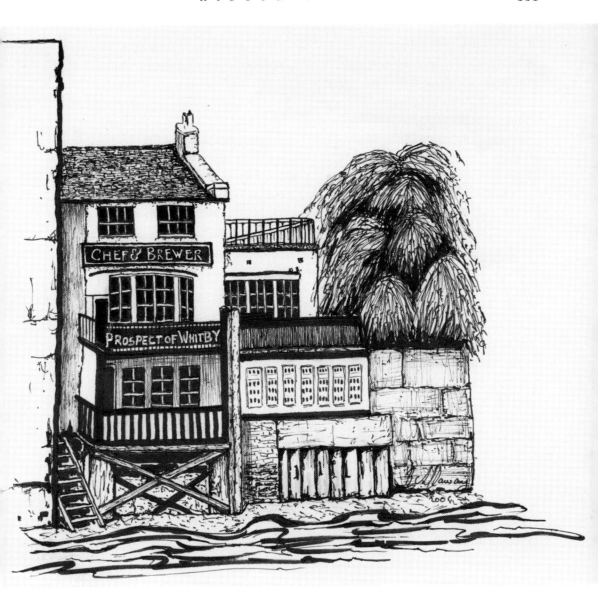

earlier days the inn was known as the Devil's Tavern, no doubt because of its dubious clientele.

Dickens used the Prospect to study the customers' faces and recreate the atmosphere in his books. Turner braved the customers here to paint the panoramic views of the Thames, as did Doré and Whistler.

Perhaps the most vividly memorable of the Prospect's patrons was Hanging Judge Jeffreys. After watching the cockfights and bare-knuckle contests upstairs, the Judge would take a seat on the terrace, where he could watch the hangings at Execution Dock. Fortified with game pie and port, he would watch some unfortunate take the drop and then, indicating the struggling offender with a chicken bone, 'All my own work,' he would quip. 'Yes, that's all my own work.'

LONDON, E14: *THE GRAPES*

The Grapes is in the aptly named Narrow Street at the Limehouse Basin.
Continue east along the A1023, The Highway, and turn right before the
Rotherhithe Tunnel Approach.

A panel on the wall of this friendly old pub shows a date of 1583. However, London historians would seem to think that the present building is nearer 1650.

This is the Limehouse area that once intrigued Dickens. It was more sordid in those days, with every type of villain that London and half of Asia could produce. This was Chinatown, home of the Limekilns, Pennyfields and the Causeway. There is an unsubstantiated story that Hare, of Burke and Hare fame, was thrown into the limepits and lost his eyesight. He re-emerged as 'The Blind Beggar', honoured by the famous pub in Whitechapel.

It is known that Dickens used the inn, and there is an ongoing argument between The Grapes and the Prospect of Whitby, both ancient hostelries claiming to be the venue that Dickens chose for 'The Six Jolly Fellowship Porters'. We shall never know.

The Grapes lies in Narrow Street, and the word is certainly applicable to the interior. It seems to be about 12 feet wide, with the wooden panelling exaggerating its lack of width. A staircase leads to the Dickens room and from there a small balcony affords some of the most spectacular views of the Thames. Whistler certainly thought so. He spent literally weeks here painting the mighty river in all its varying moods.

LONDON, SE10: *TRAFALGAR TAVERN*

The Trafalgar Tavern is in Park Row, Greenwich. South of the river again, take the A206 east, Romney Road. Park Row crosses Romney Road opposite Greenwich Park.

Greenwich is the home of the Royal Naval College, which was built on the site of the Royal Palace of Placentia. The association with the navy has gone on for centuries and the area will continue to flourish with its nautical theme thanks to the *Cutty Sark* and the National Maritime Museum.

Some 200 years ago Greenwich was a fishing village. Later, in the nineteenth century, it became busy, and was also the in-place for politicians of every persuasion, who sailed down the wide river for a whitebait supper at the Lord Nelson Room – a pleasant setting with views of the ever-broadening Thames laying siege to the Isle of Dogs.

The Trafalgar is relatively new. In 1837 it was designed and constructed by the celebrated architect Joseph Kay on the site of an older inn, The George. After a somewhat chequered financial history, the building ceased to be a pub in 1915, when it was bought by some businessmen. It was reincarnated with the prestigious name of The Royal Alfred Aged Merchant Seaman's Institute.

Thankfully, the Trafalgar Tavern re-emerged as an inn in 1965. I first visited it in the early 1970s, and when I returned in 2005 externally little had changed. The panoramic view is just as impressive, a rather pinkish rose-bowl paint has embellished some of the original white and gold decor, but overall the building has retained its charm.

There is just a little less nautical association. I remember describing the interior in a previous book. At that time: 'Upon entering one finds each side of the door the Rodney and the Hood bars, following through the Duncan and Collingwood dining rooms appear on either side. Upstairs the Hawke and Howe bar is representative of a fo'c'sle of a 1730's ship of the line.'

There is a good old nautical taste to The Trafalgar, but personally I cannot stand whitebait.

LONDON, SE10: *PILOT INN*

The Pilot Inn is on River Way, which leads towards the Millennium Dome. Continue along the A206; when it becomes Trafalgar Road, take the A2203, and look for River Way.

There is a large school of thought that regards Greenwich as the most stately part of the Thames. It is certainly steeped in history, the majestic buildings are far too numerous to mention and the number of historical characters is more plentiful still. Here walked Alfred, Cromwell, Chaucer, Milton and the famous Bard. It was here that poor old Alphege was beaten to death by the Danes. John Evelyn preached here and strolled the riverbank for hours. Here worked Inigo Jones and Christopher Wren, and there are historical associations with General Wolfe, Nelson, the famous friar William Tynsdale and Dr Johnson. Henry VIII and Elizabeth I saw the light of day at Greenwich. One could go on ad infinitum.

The Pilot Inn, at just over 200 years of age, is a little too young to have rubbed shoulders with those dignitaries mentioned above. I first heard of The Pilot by reading Peter Haydon's excellent book *The London Pub*. Peter mentions the sign of an orange-painted launch but also states that the name 'pilot' was a nickname for

(Photo: P.B. Marron)

William Pitt, on whose ground the inn was built. Personally I think that the unique geographical location of The Pilot denotes that it was named after the exceptionally skilled men who knew every creek, cranny, mudflat and tide of the river.

The building is pleasant and very busy. There is a sunken garden of some repute, which could easily be turned into a smoker's paradise when that pub-destroying act is inflicted.

On a card handed to me by the landlord, Phillip Marron, it states, 'We are the nearest inn to the Dome'. I am glad to say that Mr Marron's inn is a great deal more successful financially. Apparently it was thronged by builders during the Dome's construction and then by the artistes who followed. It is now full of ambitious young go-getters who are steadily moving in to the area.

Here's to The Pilot – a pub full of character in a very pleasant setting.

GREENHITHE VILLAGE: *PIER HOTEL*

The Pier Hotel is in the High Street of Greenhithe Village. Follow the A226 towards Gravesend in Kent. Greenhithe Village is signed on the left, and Station Road leads to the High Street.

Greenhithe has a long tradition of boats and seamen. Training ships such as the *Arethusa*, *Chichester* and *Worcester* were moored here. It has associations with Admiral Kepple and the unfortunate Sir John Franklin. A nearby pub is named after Sir John Franklin, who joined the navy at 14 and was involved at Copenhagen and Trafalgar as well as a dozen smaller skirmishes.

In 1845 Franklin, accompanied by Captain F.R.M. Crozier, set out to discover the North West Passage. Their boats, the *Erebus* and the *Terror*, sailed from Greenhithe. The expedition was a failure resulting in the demise of both crews. The deaths were brought about by starvation and scurvy, and recent television programmes suggest the possibility of cannibalism.

The Pier Hotel is snug enough for a relaxing drink beside the river. The bar has been refurbished tastefully, and the restaurant (local fish a speciality) is small but romantic, with eye-catching glimpses of the Thames. A fuller view of the river may be enjoyed from the decking outside. The proprietors have achieved that fine balance of modification without loss of character.

GRAVESEND: *NEW FALCON*

The New Falcon is on West Street, part of the A226 as it enters Gravesend. Follow the road to the left beside the river.

Crossing the water to the Kent bank we find the busy and pleasant town of Gravesend. Here the estuary becomes the river. There is a ferry to Tilbury from here, and it is the resting place of Pocahontas. The 'Native American' princess has a grave in the church and a couple of windows to commemorate her. There is also a statue, a gift from the people of Virginia, USA.

The New Falcon stands near the ferry crossing. It looks Victorian but apparently it has been here much longer. It has also been embellished by a plethora of names over the years. Before becoming The Falcon it was the Rum Butt in 1789, the Rum Puncheon in 1813 and then The Talbot in 1849.

The New Falcon is a local pub. When I called in, the colourful characters at the bar all seemed to be connected with the river in some shape or form. They seemed to know every boat on it. The bar is practical with no unnecessary decoration. The wooden floor is well in keeping with its blunt and friendly customers.

However, the main attraction is outside – the view across the river. Don't miss it.

GRAVESEND: *THREE DAWS*

The Three Daws is less than 100 yards from the New Falcon in West Street.

Another wonderful old pub in Gravesend is the Three Daws, situated by the town pier. It has been around since 1488, when it was called the Cornish Choughs. The building was part of the Page Estates. Joshua Page was a gentleman of Rochester, and James Selfe, his bailiff, was the inn's first landlord. It was here that pilgrims crossed from Essex before travelling on to Canterbury.

Although the pub has passed through countless landlords, the name remained until 1651, when ownership transferred to Thomas Scruggs, a beer-seller from Ashford. Although there was no lettering on the name board, the picture of the three Cornish choughs survived. Thinking them to be jackdaws, Scruggs registered the licence in the name of the Three Daws.

A John Knight ran the old riverside inn in the 1780s and it was during this period that the Three Daws became synonymous with smuggling. There were at least three subterranean passages. One ran from behind the chimney breast to the Fisherman's

Arms, another to the wharf and the third to St George's Church. In March 1780, after a running battle with Customs officers, 80 gallons of Geneva gin were found in the tunnels.

A second use for these passages was during the Napoleonic Wars, when sailors being pursued by press gangs used them as escape routes.

Later John Knight purchased the adjacent pilot's house as part of the inn. On inspection he found that the building had seven staircases, five of which led nowhere and were obviously placed there to confuse pursuers.

In 1821 John Knight died, passing the inn to his heirs. His granddaughter Georgina Knight ran the inn in 1856, and her grandson, Alfred Knight, took over in 1904 and kept the inn until the end of the war.

The Three Daws is now owned by Mr Lester Banks, from whom I have gleaned the above information. Mr Banks has 'sympathetically restored it to its original charm and character'. He certainly has. Try and visit it on a fine day, when the view of the river is superb.

CANVEY ISLAND: *THE HAYSTACK*

The Haystack is on Furtherwick Road, the main street through the centre of Canvey Island. Follow the A13 east until the A130 turns off to Canvey Island.

I had never been to Canvey Island so I took the opportunity of my journey to Southend to take a trip down there.

The seafront has a look of the 1950s. There is a high and very solid-looking sea wall; I imagine the tide is very high here. I walked up the main street, which was

surprisingly busy. The Haystack, a large old building on the right, was just opening. The original structure dates back to 1890, but it has been regularly altered and built onto since. Once again I was irritated and thwarted by a lack of recorded history. An inn seated in this geographical location must have a hundred colourful tales to tell, but nobody knows nowt. This being the case, I must accept defeat and merely mention the wooden floor, the banisters, the large bar-cum-restaurant and the four old gentlemen in the corner who obviously had a daily rendezvous there. At an average age of 75 there must have been 300 years of experience there somewhere.

CANVEY ISLAND: *LOBSTER SMACK*

Lobster Smack is at the end of Haven Road, a very long road in Canvey Island. It is easiest to ask for directions from the town centre.

At last, a pub with a story. The Lobster Smack is the oldest pub in the area and has a good claim at being the oldest in Essex.

A smack is a small single-sailed fishing boat, originating in Holland; it features in the overdone old saying 'It was a very stormy night and many smacks went to the bottom'.

LOBSTER SMACK

MENU

Lobster Smack Haven Road Canvey Island SS8 0NR Telephone : 01268 660021

The pub is found on the seafront at the end of the long Haven Road. Its antiquity contrasts with the stumpy gleaming towers of the adjacent oil refinery.

Outside it has typical weatherboarding, and inside the beams and low ceiling are what one might expect. Also as one might expect, it is partially a restaurant and partly a bar. The small menu card informs us that as early as 1600 there was an inn on this site. By 1700 it was rebuilt and named the World's End. Its main claim to fame is that it was the Sluice House in Dickens's novel *Great Expectations*. Sluice Farm stands a few yards along the road.

The Lobster Smack was a smugglers' haunt, its situation being conducive with the unloading of contraband. It was then loaded onto carts and delivered to the Essex towns of Hadleigh and Rayleigh: profitable work.

SOUTHEND-ON-SEA: *THE CASTLE*

The Castle is on the Seafront at Thorpe Bay. From Southend take the B1016 along the coast to Shoeburyness. Thorpe Bay is midway between the two towns.

Despite its name, Southend is on the river, not the sea. This is as far east as I go on my journey. The many-roomed and almost Gothically romantic old Castle gazes across the wide briny. It seems to have half a dozen different levels and to my uneducated guess it is mostly Victorian.

Inside it appears vast but seems to nestle into a variety of set areas. There are interesting pictures of unsmiling Victorian ladies enjoying various pursuits, such as riding bicycles and horses. And, if my memory serves me right, even trying to master golf.

I sat and ate a scrumptious steak here while gazing at a preserved copy of the *Illustrated London News*. I then washed my meal down with a large Scotch and studied pictures of *Fishing at Eastbourne*, *Cockle Gathering in Essex* and *Bass Fishing on the South Coast*. It would take several hours to investigate every corner of this intriguing old pub. I am sure it could tell many a captivating story. As in many cases though, regretfully nothing has been recorded.

Just one piece of more modern information before I leave. A newspaper extract on the wall informs us that The Castle possesses the record for the youngest landlady ever – a slip of a girl of 18.

Journey's end, and a satisfying job done.

BIBLIOGRAPHY

Atterbury, Paul, and Haines, Anthony, *The Thames* (London: Cassell, 2002)

Camp, John, *Oxfordshire and Buckinghamshire Pubs* (London: B.T. Batsford, 1965)

Haydon, Peter, and Coe, Chris, *The London Pub* (London: New Holland, 2003)

Keeble, Richard, *Surrey Pubs* (London: B.T. Batsford, 1965)

Mee, Arthur, *The King's England: Oxfordshire* (London: Caxton, 1945)

—— *The King's England: Buckinghamshire* (London: Caxton, n.d.)

Middleton, Tom, *Royal Berkshire* (Buckingham: Barracuda Books, 1979)

Millison, Cecilia, *Tales of Old Oxfordshire* (Newbury: Countryside Books, n.d.)

Ronay, Egon, *Pub Guides* (London: Egon Ronay Publications, 1985)

Roulstone, Alan, and Roulstone, Michael, *Taverns in Town* (St Ives: Balfour/Travellers Rest Publications, 1973)

Smith, Jacqueline, and Carter, John, *Inns and Alehouses of Abingdon* (Abingdon: Smith & Carter, 1978)

The Women's Institute, *Old Berkshire Village Book* (Newbury: Countryside Books, n.d.)

ACKNOWLEDGEMENTS

I am grateful to Brenda Allaway, for photographs and artwork; to Dave Blackman for help compiling this book; to Simon Fletcher for his advice and for photographs; and to Tom Walford for photographs.

INDEX OF INNS